Red Hat and IT Security

With Red Hat Ansible, Red Hat OpenShift, and Red Hat Security Auditing

Rithik Chatterjee

Apress®

Red Hat and IT Security

Rithik Chatterjee
Pune, Maharashtra, India

ISBN-13 (pbk): 978-1-4842-6433-1   ISBN-13 (electronic): 978-1-4842-6434-8
https://doi.org/10.1007/978-1-4842-6434-8

Managing Director, Apress Media LLC: Welmoed Spahr
Acquisitions Editor: Divya Modi
Development Editor: Matthew Moodie
Coordinating Editor: Divya Modi

Cover designed by eStudioCalamar

Cover image designed by Pixabay

Distributed to the book trade worldwide by Springer Science+Business Media New York, 1 New York Plaza, Suite 4600, New York, NY 10004-1562, USA. Phone 1-800-SPRINGER, fax (201) 348-4505, e-mail orders-ny@springer-sbm.com, or visit www.springeronline.com. Apress Media, LLC is a California LLC and the sole member (owner) is Springer Science + Business Media Finance Inc (SSBM Finance Inc). SSBM Finance Inc is a **Delaware** corporation.

For information on translations, please e-mail booktranslations@springernature.com; for reprint, paperback, or audio rights, please e-mail bookpermissions@springernature.com.

Apress titles may be purchased in bulk for academic, corporate, or promotional use. eBook versions and licenses are also available for most titles. For more information, reference our Print and eBook Bulk Sales web page at http://www.apress.com/bulk-sales.

Any source code or other supplementary material referenced by the author in this book is available to readers on GitHub via the book's product page, located at www.apress.com/978-1-4842-6433-1. For more detailed information, please visit http://www.apress.com/source-code.

Printed on acid-free paper

This book is dedicated to my parents: Rita and Ashish; thank you for always supporting and encouraging me to pursue my ambitions.

Table of Contents

About the Author

 **Rithik Chatterjee** graduated as an electronics and telecommunications engineer. As he was interested in the networking domain, he completed his course in IT infrastructure management and later became accredited as a Red Hat Certified System Administrator and Red Hat Certified Engineer. Working for a startup, his responsibilities included network/system administration, IT security, information security, and DevOps. Having gained a better understanding of the IT landscape, his interest and goals started to lean toward cybersecurity, leading him to his training and certification as an EC-Council Certified Ethical Hacker.

His hobbies include landscape and wildlife photography, blogging, reading, and watching anime. To pursue his hobby of writing, he developed his own blogging website (Inspirio Scripts), also encouraging budding authors like him to pen their thoughts.

About the Technical Reviewer

 **Himanshu Tank** has a B. Tech in computer
Science. He is an open source enthusiast and
a Red Hat Certified Architect in Infrastructures
(RHCA)-Level 1 certified professional. He
is extremely knowledgeable about core
products by Red Hat such as Ansible,
OpenShift, OpenStack, CEPH Storage, Linux
TroubleShooting and Diagnostics, Server
Security, and Hardening.

Acknowledgments

I would like to thank my uncles: Tapas and Subarna for being my secondary guardians, and to my close friends for being a part of my journey.

I extend my gratitude toward Nishant for dragging me into this domain, Prajakta ma'am for being a wonderful teacher, and Priyanshu for assisting me with the graphics.

This book would not have been possible without Divya who provided me with the opportunity, and Matthew and Himanshu who imparted their valuable insights into this project; thank you.

A special thanks to Shraddha, Pratiksha, and Kiran for your incredible support and being my sounding boards.

Introduction

This book is intended for IT professionals in the domains of network and system administration, IT infrastructure, cybersecurity, DevOps, CISO, and similar profiles.

Security is, more often than not, a neglected aspect in the IT industry. Organizations fail to realize the significance of a secure infrastructure environment and tend to invest only in the bare essentials. Traditional infrastructure sure gets the job done but in the current day and age, it is not enough to tackle evolving cyber threats. Numerous organizations have had to pay the price for their carefree attitude toward security administration.

This book intends to cover the basic, intermediate, and a few advanced concepts related to infrastructure security and how to enhance this security using certain Red Hat solutions. Traditional infrastructure sure gets the job done, but in these times, it is not enough to tackle evolving cyber threats. Readers can consider this as an informative guide on developing and implementing secure controls and configurations in various environments, including physical data centers, virtualization, and cloud environments.

Red Hat and IT Security has been written with the sole intention of providing information to readers that are usually not highlighted enough even with the rise in modern technologies. Most of the books available are domain specific like Red Hat / Linux, IT infrastructure, Cybersecurity, or DevOps. However, this book transcends the barriers and amalgamates all these fields to provide a distinct yet comprehensible insight into the overall world of Red Hat and IT Security, hence the name.

CHAPTER 1

Introduction to IT Security

To build or maintain any secure and sturdy IT (Information Technology) infrastructure, you need to be familiar with and have a working understanding of the basics pertaining to computer networking, system administration, and primary security aspects. This chapter will cover the essential concepts deemed necessary for you to gain a better understanding of security in RHEL (Red Hat Enterprise Linux) and information contained in the following chapters. As almost all administrators are acquainted with the core basics of networking and system administration, this chapter will focus more on the intermediate topics that you will probably want to learn about and might occasionally search for on the internet.

Basics of Networking

It is critical for every IT infrastructure to have a reliable networking backbone. All IT professionals are more or less familiar with the networking basics like the OSI model, IP network, interfaces, and so on. However, there are a few technical concepts that many novices are unaware of, mostly due to their lack of practical exposure. It is not always necessary to know all such concepts in depth, but one should at least be aware of the basic overview that is required while working in the network/system administration domain.

© Rithik Chatterjee 2021
R. Chatterjee, *Red Hat and IT Security*,
https://doi.org/10.1007/978-1-4842-6434-8_1

Firewalls

Firewalls are programs that are responsible for filtering and routing network traffic. Each packet request is analysed and then either validated or dropped. It can be configured to monitor all incoming and outgoing packets for any unapproved or suspicious activities. The user needs to create rules to determine the type of traffic that will be allowed and on which particular ports. Unused ports on a server are usually blocked by the firewall.

Virtual Private Network

A VPN (Virtual Private Network) is used to create an online private network connection linking sites or users from remote locations. These virtual connections are routed across the internet from an organization's private network or server to ensure secure and encrypted data transfer. A VPN masks the IP address, thus also providing users with anonymity while maintaining privacy. After connecting to a VPN, your data traffic is encoded and transferred through a secure tunneled connection. The VPN server then decrypts the data and sends it over the internet. Upon receiving a response, the server then encrypts the data and transmits it back to you, which the VPN software on your system decrypts.

Virtual Private Cloud

A VPC (Virtual Private Cloud) is a scalable virtual cloud environment on public cloud infrastructure that enables organizations to develop an isolated configurable private network. This virtual private network is logically isolated by assigning a private IP subnet, VLAN, and a secure VPN to each user. The network and security configurations are used to control the access of resources by specified IP addresses or applications. The cloud resources are generally classified into three categories: Networking, Computing, and Storage. VPCs are usually preferred in Infrastructure as a Service for the cloud.

DHCP

The network protocol DHCP (Dynamic Host Configuration Protocol), allows a server to automatically assign IP addresses to systems from a predefined scope of an IP range allocated to a particular network. Additionally, a DHCP server is also responsible for assigning the subnet mask, default gateway, and DNS address. The IP addresses are sequentially assigned from lowest to highest. While connecting to a network, the client broadcasts a DISCOVER request, which is routed to the DHCP server. Depending on the configuration and the IP addresses available, the server assigns an IP address to the system and reserves it while sending the client an OFFER packet consisting of the details of the IP address. A REQUEST packet is then sent by the client to mention its usage of the IP address. The server then provides the client with an ACK packet as a confirmation of the leased IP address for a time period defined by the server.

Domain Name System

A DNS (Domain Name System) is a stratified method for the naming of systems and resources connected through a public or private network. It is used to convert the alphabetic or alphanumeric domain names into their respective IP addresses. When a domain name like *xyz.com* is used to access a specific website, a DNS server translates that domain name into the IP address associated with it. Each system on the internet requires an IP address to communicate with each other, which can be tedious for humans to memorize while multiple IP addresses can also be associated to a single domain name, which can later also be modified over time. Through DNS name resolution, a DNS server resolves the domain name to its respective IP address.

TCP

TCP (Transmission Control Protocol) enables the trading of information among systems in a network. Information from a system is fragmented into packets that are then routed by network devices like switches and routers to its destination. Each packet is numbered and reassembled before providing them to the recipient. TCP is a reliable source to transmit data while ensuring that data is delivered in the exact order it was originally sent. TCP establishes a connection and it is maintained until the data transfer is completed. Because of unreliable network fluctuations, IP packets can be dropped or lost during the transmission. TCP is responsible for identifying and reducing such issues by sequencing the packets or requesting the sender to retransmit the data packet. This precision reliability impedes the speed of the data transfer, which is why UDP is preferred when speed is highly prioritized.

UDP

Dissimilar to TCP, UDP (User Datagram Protocol) is a connectionless protocol making it unreliable, which it makes up for with reduced latency. UDP quickens the data transmission process as it does not require a 'handshake', which allows UDP to drop delayed packets instead of processing them. UDP does not facilitate any error checking or packet sequencing, which also leads to reduced bandwidth usage. Real-time applications like DNS, NTP, VoIP, video communication, and online gaming, use UDP to ensure efficiency and low latency. However, the unreliability of the protocol also exposes it to cybersecurity threats that are often leveraged by attackers.

Simple Network Management Protocol

Part of the TCP/IP suite, the SNMP (Simple Network Management Protocol) works in the application layer, used to monitor and modify data across all network devices. SNMP can be used to identify network issues while also configuring the devices remotely. There are three main elements required for proper functioning of the protocol.

- **SNMP Manager**

    Also referred to as the Network Management Station, this system enables monitoring and communication through the network devices configured by the SNMP agent. It's primary functions include querying agents, retrieving responses from them, variable setting, and agent asynchronous event acknowledgment.

- **SNMP Agent**

    The SNMP agent is responsible for storing, collecting, and retrieving management information and provides it back to the SNMP manager. These agents could either be open source or proprietary depending on the specifications. The agent could also act as a proxy for a few network nodes that are unmanageable by SNMP.

- **Managed Devices**

    These devices are part of the network structure that need to be monitored, managed, and accordingly configured. Devices like switches, routers, servers, printers, and similar items are examples.

- **Management Information Base (MIB)**

  MIB is a stack of hierarchically organized information used to manage network resources. It includes manageable objects (Scalar and Tabular) that use a unique Object Identifier or OID to denote and recognize them. These objects can also be considered variables.

SSH

Commonly known as SSH, Secure Shell is an administration protocol that enables users to access, monitor, and configure a remote server directly through the internet or via VPN tunneling. Meant to replace the unsecured Telnet protocol, SSH provides authentication and authenticity to ensure encrypted communication. Users are required to install an OpenSSH server on the system they will access to, and an OpenSSH client on the system they will access it from. While Windows users can use OpenSSH client through applications like PuTTY (or add the OpenSSH client feature from *Manage Optional Features* option available in Windows 10), Linux and macOS users can utilize their default terminal to access a server by SSH using the command-line interface. SSH makes use of three types of encryption technologies: Symmetrical encryption, Asymmetrical encryption, and Hashing.

HTTP

The HTTP (HyperText Transfer Protocol) is the fundamental stateless protocol used for data transfer in the World Wide Web. Part of the TCP/IP suite, HTTP specifies requests, services, and commands generally utilized to transmit a website's data. The media independence feature of HTTP enables it to transfer all sorts of data, provided both the server and client are capable of handling the data type. Commands like GET and POST are also defined by HTTP to process the website form submissions. To enhance security, connections through HTTP are encrypted using SSL or TLS. These encrypted data transfers are carried out over HTTPS, designed as a secure extension over the standard HTTP protocol. HTTP connections use default port 80, while the secure connections over HTTPS use the default port 443.

SSL/TLS

Secure Socket Layer or commonly referred to as SSL was developed to provide secure and encrypted communications over the internet, which is now considered obsolete. The transiting data is scrambled using an encryption algorithm of asymmetrical cryptography to prevent data leakage. SSL has had several security flaws despite releasing multiple versions. To overcome these existing security issues of SSL, the Transport Layer Security (TLS) protocol was developed. Unlike its predecessor, TLS uses asymmetric cryptography only to generate the initial session key. As a single shared key is used for encryption by both server and client, it is termed as symmetric cryptography, which reduces the overall computational overhead. Due to this, TLS provides more secure connections with low latency.

Network Address Translation

Network Address Translation (NAT) allows using a single public IP address by numerous devices in a private network. Operating on a router, NAT connects the private network to the internet by translating the individual private addresses of the network into globally unique registered addresses. With configuration, NAT can be used to broadcast the same IP address for all systems in a network, over the internet. This enables more secure data transfer for a network by representing all the systems of the network by a single IP address. NAT additionally helps to avoid address exhaustion (IPv4).

Port Forwarding

Port forwarding is used to reroute a connection from a specific IP address associated with a port number to another such combination. While data is in transmission, the packet header is read by the application or device configured to intercept the traffic, which then rescripts the header data to send it to the mapped destination address. Servers can be prevented from undesired access by concealing the services and applications on the network, to redirect all the traffic to a different IP and port combination. As port forwarding is a NAT application, it also helps in address preservation and provides upgraded network security.

IT Infrastructure Elements

Switching vs. Routing

In switching, data packets are transmitted to devices within the same network. Operating at layer 2 (Data Link Layer) of the OSI model, switches discern the packet destination by analyzing the packet header consisting of the MAC address of the destination system. Switches create and manage a database consisting of indexed data of MAC addresses and its connected ports. Switches are generally categorized as managed or unmanaged. Unmanaged switches do not allow any modifications in its functioning, making it viable for home networks. Managed switches enable access and deeper control to determine the traffic flow across the network, which can also be monitored remotely.

Contrarily, in routing, packets can be transmitted over various networks too. Routers function at layer 3 (Network Layer) of the OSI model and unlike switches, it controls the packet destination through the Network ID included in the network layer header. Network traffic is analysed by routers, configures it if required, and securely transmits it across another network. Routers work like a dispatcher: using the routing table, it decides the most appropriate packet route for prompt data travel. Modern routers also have enhanced features like a built-in firewall, VPN, and even IP telephony network.

Domain Controller

Used for network security, a Domain Controller (DC) is responsible for authenticating and authorizing user controls. With multiple systems connected in a domain, when a user logs into the network, a DC validates data like name, password, privileges related to the group, and individual policies defined in the server. DCs provide a centralized user management system, which also enables users to share resources securely. As DCs are more suitable for on-prem data centers, Directory as a Service is a better alternative for cloud users. Although DCs are more prone to cyber-attacks, this can be prevented by server hardening and regular updating for enhanced security.

Database Server

As the name implies, a database server is used to store the data of an organization that can be accessed and modified whenever required. It maintains the DBMS (Database Management System) along with all the databases. As per the received requests from users, systems, or servers, the Database Server probes for the associated data from all its databases and provides it back to the requested user. Used more often in a server-client architecture, a Database Server executes operations like data storage, access and modification, data archiving, and data analysis among other back-end tasks.

Application Server

An application server is responsible for handling all application-related operations, which often include both hardware and appropriate software required for the tasks. It is usually preferred for intricate transactional applications like payment gateways or accounting. Thus to provide effortless performance and bear the computational overhead, application servers have features like prebuilt redundancy, constant monitoring, pooling of resources, scalability, and more. There can also be other uses of an app server like a web application server, virtual machine host, patching and inspecting software updates across a network, or a transitional data processing server.

Load Balancing Server

A load balancing server is responsible for coherently distributing the network traffic over collective back-end servers of a data center. Load balancers are strategically connected as an intermediary server that receives the incoming traffic and evenly administers it across multiple servers. It improves the overall functionality, especially of applications with microservices. Load balancers make use of algorithms and methods like Round Robin, Weighted Round Robin, Chained Failover, Source IP Hash, URL Hash, Global Server Load Balancing, Least Connection, and Weighted Response Time, each having its distinct features catering to various requirements.

Linux System Administration Essential Concepts

System administration in Linux is a very wide domain that primarily requires command-line proficiency. Hence, to cover the basics pertinent to Linux, would require a whole book in itself. So this chapter is intended to highlight only the critical aspects of Linux that you need to know about before proceeding to the next chapters.

Directory Services

Directory services can be defined as a network service that acts as a unified repository associating all the network resources to make them accessible for the applications, services, and users. All kinds of data can be stored that are relevant to an organization, which is mostly used for user authorization and authentication by determining secure access to the available resources. Simplifying the network structure, Directory services enable users to remotely access the resources despite being unaware of its physical connection.

LDAP

The open protocol: LDAP (Lightweight Directory Access Protocol), is primarily utilized as a centralized database to help store, access, and retrieve information across a network. Varied information related to an organization is stored in this database like a directory service. LDAP is responsible for the data representation of a directory service to the users, while also defining conditions for the elements, using the data entries in a directory service where they are created.

LDAP works based on a server-client model, similar to many networking protocols. Initially, an LDAP client requests a connection to the LDAP server. Based on the configured privileges and accessibility, the server is responsible for accepting or denying the request. If accepted, the client can query, access, or browse the data stored in the directory service, which can also be modified if the client has sufficient privileges.

It is important to understand the primary data components of LDAP that are used to represent the data to its users based on the interactivity between these components.

- **Attributes**

    These are elements used to store the data in LDAP. Akin to pairs of key values, attributes have keys with preset names governed by LDAP object classes. Usually attribute values consist of user or organization information like mail, address, or phone numbers. A sample of a mail attribute would be like the following:

    ```
    mail: user@organization.com
    ```

- **Entries**

    An entry can be defined as a heap of stacked attributes within a set name. Per entry includes three basic elements starting with a *distinguished name (dn)* followed by a set of *attributes* and *object classes*.

    ```
    dn: uid=user,ou=marketing,dc=organization,dc=com
    ```

- **Schema**

    Schema files are a set of rules that define the directory system and its contents. Schemas consist of object class definitions and attribute type definitions among other data. A few samples of schemas are *core. schema, LDIF (LDAP Data Interchange Format)*, and *organizationalPerson.*

- **Object Class**

    Object classes can be described as stacked piles of attribute types used to describe a certain unit. These schema elements indicate the type of objects represented in entries while also listing a group of the required and optional attribute types. Each object in LDAP requires an objectclass attribute.

```
dn: uid=user,ou=marketing,dc=organization,dc=com
objectClass: employee
```

File Systems in Linux

Despite Linux kernels being able to detect raw storage, the drives cannot be used in their default state. It is necessary to write a file system to the drive through the formatting process in order to utilize it for system operational tasks. A file system enables organizing the data and modulating the way information is compiled and recovered through the storage disk. With various file system formats, each has its own features including cross-platform compatibility. Mentioned below are the widely used file systems in Linux.

- **Ext**

  The Extended file system has been the most popular file system of Linux for a long time. The original and first version of ext is now deprecated, while the ext2 was the first file system in Linux to allow 2Tb data operations and ext3 was just its upgraded version with some fixes. The fourth version of ext, that is, ext4 is the currently used file system as it is much faster and can handle large file sizes with high speed. ext4 is a journaling file system with backward compatibility and stability. Hence it is the preferred and default option recommended by Linux during installation, especially for SSD storages.

- **XFS**

    Designed for better performance and handling huge
    data files, XFS performs just metadata journaling,
    unlike ext4 that uses both metadata and data. Although
    this provides faster operations, this could also lead to
    probable data corruption during events like a power
    cut. An XFS file system can be formatted rapidly and
    has decent output features while controlling vast
    files and disks. The biggest flaw of XFS is that it is
    very slow while handling small data files and is not
    recommended for such operations.

- **Btrfs (B-Tree File System)**

    Considered as a latest feature-packed file system, Btrfs
    provides features like snapshots, managing logical
    volumes, cloning, and more. Despite having a few
    issues like handling full drives and overall stability,
    Btrfs can be considered a valid replacement for ext if
    required, due to its optimum performance.

- **ZFS**

    This copy-on-write file system is very sturdy and well-
    developed with its varied features. ZFS has pooled
    storage along with being able to verify data integrity
    and auto-repair. Volumes can be organized in RAID-Z
    and similar arrays to boost the functionality. Due to its
    limited support availability, ZFS is mostly preferred by
    advanced users for specific requirements.

Block Storage

In networking, a block is specified as a physical record every so often, and it is actually a byte/bit sequence consisting of entire records with a maximum length of a block size. Block storage, which is also known as block-level storage, is a storage system utilized for storing data files in either cloud environments or SANs (Storage Area Networks). In block storage, data is segregated and stored into isolated blocks, each with a unique identifier. This helps the storage system to determine the placement of smaller data blocks as per convenience. Due to this, data storage in cross-platform environments is possible too. Administrators are now preferring block storage to meet their quick, coherent, and stable data transfer and storage requirements. Block storage configuration enables users for decoupling data from their own environment and expands it over different environments for higher efficiency. Upon a data request, the core storage software reorganizes the data collected from all such environments and provides it back to the requested application or user.

Security Basics in Linux

Access Control Lists (ACLs)

In order to ensure data security and prevent unauthorised access, you can set file permissions in Linux with commands like *chown, chmod*, and *chgrp* but they do not provide adequate security due to its limitations. An access control list or ACL provides an enhanced permission process for the files and directories. ACL enables granting permission to users or groups for required disk resources. To give you a better idea, suppose you need to give write permission to a particular user without adding that user to a group with such preexisting permissions. Using ACL, you can provide the user with an individual write permission. The command to do so would be like the following:

```
# setfacl -m u:user:rwx /file/path
```

To view the ACL permissions of a file you can use the following command:

```
# getfacl xyz.txt
```

Default ACLs are similar; they do not change the overall directory permissions but instead enable the default activations of the defined ACLs on all files created within the folders. The command for the same would look like this:

```
# mkdir xyz && setfacl -d -m u:user:rw xyz
```

SELinux

Primary-level file permissions and access control lists still persist with limitations like accidentally exposing a file/folder to a security threat due to an ill-defined command of *chmod* or *chown*, causing an unprecedented spiraling of access rights. Hence all processes initiated by such a user will have elevated privileges that may cause malware or similar compromised applications to gain root access of the system. To overcome such security limitations, SELinux (Security-Enhanced Linux) was designed by the NSA (National Security Agency) to provide an imperative and versatile access control process that restricts access and privileges of processes to prevent them from altering any system entities.

SELinux applies security policies that are used to specify access controls for files, processes, and programs of a system. The SELinux policies dictate the access rights to enforce it systemwide. The process works when a subject (process or application) requests access to an object (file/folder); it then leads SELinux to verify from its Access Vector Cache (AVC), a permission cache register of subjects and objects. In an indecisive event by SELinux, the request is forwarded to the security server, which scans the security context of the subject and object. The SELinux policy database determines the applied security context, based on which permission is either denied or granted.

SELinux can operate in one of these three mentioned modes:

- **Enforcing**

  Depending on the SELinux policies, it denies access to users and applications unless the security policies permit otherwise. The denial notifications are logged as AVC denials.

- **Permissive**

  In this mode, there is no enforcing of the security policies as this works as a diagnostic state. SELinux informs the user about what would have been denied access, had it been in the enforcing mode. The denial messages are sent to the log file.

- **Disabled**

  In this mode, no security policies are enforced or implemented as none are stacked in the kernel. DAC (Discretionary Access Control) rules take precedence as default access control.

You can set the SELinux modes in multiple ways, either by selecting the mode from the status view of the SELinux GUI or by modifying the primary config file of SELinux.

```
# vim /etc/selinux/config
SELINUX=enforcing
```

You can also set the modes between enforcing and permissive by using the *setenforce* command; however, the mode would not be setting permanently, unpersisting post reboots. To set into the enforcing mode, use this command:

```
# setenforce 1
```

To set into permissive mode, use this command:

```
# setenforce 0
```

To display the current SELinux mode, use this command:

```
# getenforce
```

Firewall Daemon (Firewalld)

Previous Linux firewall mechanisms (iptables) needed to be restarted to apply any changes made, which disconnected all functioning connections. The introduction of Firewalld resolved that issue along with providing the feature of dynamic zones enabling users to configure various zones with different rules, like your home and work network or public and private zone. Zones can be assigned to the interfaces through the Network Manager, firewall-config tool or from CLI. To list all the available zones use the following commands:

```
# firewall-cmd --get-zones
# firewall-cmd --list-all-zones
```

To view the default or active zone, use the commands:

```
# firewall-cmd --get-default-zone
# firewall-cmd --get-active-zones
```

In case you prefer using the GUI to make firewall changes, use the following command to install it:

```
# yum install firewalld firewall-config
```

Prior to implementing the firewalld rules, ensure that the firewall service is installed, enabled, and running. You can use the below-mentioned command to check its status:

```
# systemctl status firewalld
```

Ports may not be open by default depending on the zone rules. To open a port in the work zone, use the following command:

```
# firewall-cmd --permanent --zone=work --add-port=22/ssh
```

Likewise, to remove the added port, use the firewalld command specified below:

```
# firewall-cmd --zone=work --remove-port=22/ssh
```

To confirm the adding or removal of ports and view them, use the below command:

```
# firewall-cmd --zone=work --list-ports
```

Firewalld already has built-in rules with preset services, so to add additional services as per the requirement, you either will have to list the services in a fresh XML file or manually specify each service through commands. The commands to add and remove service are similar to those of adding ports as mentioned above.

```
# firewall-cmd --zone=work --add-service=tcp
# firewall-cmd --zone=work --remove-service=tcp
```

To view the firewalld services of a zone, use the command:

```
# firewall-cmd --zone=work --list-services
```

Standardizing Security in Network and System Administration

Information security is a critical aspect of cybersecurity that deserves equal attention and efforts, especially by system administrators. Security specialists and organizations worldwide follow the standard of the CIA (Confidentiality, Integrity, Availability) triad. Considered as three of the most important security components that define the information security policies of organizations, the CIA triad emphasizes on infosec (information security) without impeding productivity.

Confidentiality

The Confidentiality principle determines the access control of information throughout the organization. It is intended to restrict access to unapproved personnel while maintaining access for authorized people. Data is sorted depending on it's type and sensitivity. Therefore, policies should be implemented defining strict measures if such data is exposed to unwanted people. Strong passwords, multi-factor authentication, and data encryption can be executed to enhance data confidentiality.

Integrity

The Integrity component provides assurance that the data is authentic and reliable. Sensitive and critical data should not be modified without absolute requirements and prior written approval of senior management. Strict security policies should be in place to tackle any such unapproved data alteration along with access restrictions to prevent this from happening in the first place. In case of data corruption or modification due to system failure, server crash, external security breach, and similar technical or natural causes, backup and recovery policies must be implemented.

Availability

The Availability principle of the triad focuses on ensuring constant and uninterrupted access to critical data for authorized users. Efficient maintenance and organizing the data are very helpful in providing the availability of data whenever required. Secure communication channels, backup and recovery, RAID server, and load balancing are a few implementations that can increase data availability for users. Policies for events like cybersecurity breaches, power failures, and network downtimes should be taken into account to avoid productivity loss due to data unavailability. It is also essential to have a Disaster Recovery Plan to avoid critical data loss in case of a disastrous event.

## CHAPTER 2

Red Hat Hybrid Cloud Infrastructure

This chapter aims to highlight the key concepts and technologies related to cloud infrastructure and Red Hat cloud environment solutions.

Basics of Cloud Infrastructure

Every organization creates or manages large magnitudes of data that they need storage for. Many small-scale businesses, especially startups, cannot afford to have an on-prem IT infrastructure, let alone a private data center. You would also have to ensure the optimum security of the infrastructure at all times as per the security standards to stay clear of potential data breaches or cybersecurity threats. This is why cloud computing remains a very efficient, affordable, and convenient option for most organizations. While meeting the scalable computational requirements with lower maintenance costs, cloud infrastructure also increases productivity and accessibility.

What Is Cloud Computing?

Cloud computing involves a wide variety of services ranging from storage, networking, and computing, to data processing and artificial intelligence. Basically, almost all the services required by organizations to replace a

© Rithik Chatterjee 2021
R. Chatterjee, *Red Hat and IT Security*,
https://doi.org/10.1007/978-1-4842-6434-8_2

physical data center can be carried out through these cloud services. You already must be using a few basic cloud applications like cloud storage by Google Drive or iCloud. Even media streaming platforms like *Netflix* are reliant on cloud infrastructure for most of its operations, which indicates how reliable cloud computing is. Organizations have the freedom of paying and using only the resources that they need, which is also scalable even on a real-time basis.

There are several benefits of using a cloud infrastructure that organizations evaluate before deciding to switch over to cloud computing over building a private IT infrastructure. The cost to rent an infrastructure component or a service is significantly lower than setting up hardware or software for the same purpose. Remember, organizations will only have to pay for the resources they utilize and for the time period they use it. Performance can also be enhanced or degraded as per the convenience of the users, which makes cloud computing incredibly scalable. Just by providing the specifications and configurations, you will be allocated the service or component that usually would take days to set up physically, and the same goes for up-gradation, which can be automated in cloud infrastructure. The maintenance costs and issues are also drastically decreased as it is entirely the responsibility of the cloud vendor. Even security is managed by the service providers, albeit it also depends on your defined configurations. With benefits like automated backup and recovery, frequent software updates, secure data storage, and cross-platform compatibility, it is no wonder that an increasing number of companies are now preferring cloud infrastructure for their requirements.

Having said that, cloud infrastructure also has a few drawbacks that can be considered or ignored based on the specific preferences of every organization. The most common ones include a mandatory internet connection since all activities will be performed on the cloud, privacy risk, vulnerability in case of any cyber-attack on the service provider, deviation of compliance, and a few more.

Depending on your business necessities, you can choose from the three main types of cloud infrastructure models.

- **Public Cloud**

  In public clouds, users are able to access varied cloud computing resources. A public cloud provides cloud computing services like virtualization, development applications, premium infrastructure, expandable storage, and much more. These services are run on physical data centers and server farms owned by the cloud vendors; hence they bear the entire responsibility of maintenance, a network with high bandwidths, and security. Based on the individual requirements of each user, the shared resources can also be scaled to fine-tune the performance of services. These resources are shared among numerous users, referred to as multi-tenant architecture. This means, although each user's data is logically segregated, multiple users may share the same physical server simultaneously for its resources. As the resources are shared across multiple users, public cloud tends to be quite cost efficient compared to other cloud models.

- **Private Cloud**

  Providing the perks of public cloud while maintaining the authority over services, data, configuration, and security, this is what Private Cloud entails. Unlike public clouds, there is only a single tenant in a private cloud infrastructure. A private cloud can be both off-site or on-site, providing an extra layer of security through the firewall of the tenant organization and the cloud service provider. Virtualization is the core technology in private clouds, which merges resources deriving from hardware infrastructure into shared reserves. Apart from handling expanding computations, resources can also be allocated efficiently.

- **Hybrid Cloud**

  Hybrid clouds are a combination of multiple cloud environments, mostly public and private, with specific features from both of them. An increasing number of organizations are preferring hybrid clouds due to their flexibility. Fluctuating needs for computation, networking, and storage encourage organizations to use hybrid clouds. It enables users to logically scale their on-prem infrastructure to a public cloud for managing any workloads. Many companies often choose to use the computation or storage scalability of the public cloud for secondary tasks while reserving the on-prem private cloud environment for their primary essential tasks to ensure a balance between security and convenience. This orchestration provides organizations with the required flexibility to decide for themselves the favorable cloud environment for each application or service.

Cloud Computing Services

Cloud computing enables organizations to use resources and applications provided by cloud service vendors from their own data centers via the internet. This ease of accessibility encourages users to opt for cloud services instead of investing in on-prem infrastructure and employees to manage and secure the hardware and components. Apart from cost efficiency and agility, organizations can deploy a high-grade data center in minutes instead of spending weeks and months for a physical one. Before mentioning the main types of cloud services, it is important to know about a few common noteworthy factors that define them.

- **On-Demand basis**

  Resources and services are provided to users as per the on-demand basis of requirements, which can fluctuate even in runtime environments. Instead of providing resources with high-end configurations right from the start, on-demand service allows users to utilize them as and when needed.

- **Virtualization**

  Virtualization in cloud computing is creating a virtual environment for a server, operating systems, or storage devices. Apart from being able to use multiple systems simultaneously, the same physical resource can be shared among several users. There are four types of virtualization in cloud computing: Hardware, Operating System, Server, and Storage.

- **Accessibility**

  Cloud services or resources can be accessed from various devices like computers, smartphones, or tablets either through web interfaces (browsers) or client applications. Most cloud service vendors allow users to access their services or resources irrespective of the device or location; as long as it is secure, all you would need is an active internet connection.

- **Tenancy**

  Cloud computing involves single and multi-tenancy, depending on the cloud model and service chosen. Public cloud offers multi-tenancy implying several users utilize the same physical resource but are logically isolated. Whereas private clouds provide higher control and flexibility by offering single tenancy, which lets users have their own resource with access to no one else and all security and configurations can be controlled by a single organization.

- **Scalability**

  Scalability in cloud computing enables users to scale up or down the service, resource, or application being used. Aspects like CPU, memory, network, or disk can be expanded or reduced to meet the requirements. There are two ways of scaling in cloud computing: Vertical and Horizontal Scaling. In Vertical scaling, users can enhance the power of an instance like increasing or decreasing the RAM, storage, or CPU cores. Horizontal scaling enables users to divide the increasing overload across more systems by increasing the number of servers/machines, like a load balancer.

- **Metered Billing**

  Reporting tools in the cloud keep track of all the usage and activities of an organization or user, through which the cloud service vendors measure the utilization based on which users are billed. Organizations receive alerts via notifications or emails, which provide detailed statistics of services/resources used, the time used for each, and the configurations for each of those. All of these factors determine the meter use by which the billing is calculated.

Cloud computing services can be categorized into three main types of models as follows:

Infrastructure as a Service (IaaS)

IaaS provides organizations virtual access to resources like computational processing, clusters, load balancers, storage, security, network interconnectivity, IP addresses, or basically everything you would need to build a physical data center. An entire IT infrastructure ecosystem for an organization could be developed through this cloud service. IaaS enables users to develop secure and scalable infrastructure while providing automation and total control. The virtual environment provided to users is derived from resources spread throughout several servers and networks over multiple data centers. Acting like a failsafe, this ensures that the service will be kept reliable, secure, and redundant. Organizations like startups benefit a lot from this service, which not only saves the hassle of building physical on-prem infrastructure but also helps with cost effectiveness, convenience, and accessibility. Google Compute Engine (GCE), Amazon Elastic Compute Cloud (EC2), Amazon Virtual Private Cloud (VPC), Microsoft Azure IaaS, and Cisco UCS Director are some of the well-known examples of IaaS used by many organizations.

Platform as a Service (PaaS)

PaaS provides an integrated environment for developers to deploy applications and also perform testing and support for them. Whatever resources users would need to create, operate, and maintain a web application, is provided as a cloud service via the internet. To provide users with access to the latest technologies for their platform, services receive regular updates along with increasing features by cloud vendors to stay competitive. Software and web developers prefer this service. Good examples of PaaS systems are Google App Engine, Salesforce PaaS, Microsoft Azure SQL, AWS Elastic Beanstalk, and Red Hat OpenShift.

Some cloud vendors even allow you to use PaaS for almost a negligible cost, to help you get started with developing your application. It also provides a high amount of scalability; however, a limitation of PaaS is that of scrutinizing data security and implementing all the appropriate security controls. Users are billed based on how the applications are used on the platform.

Software as a Service (SaaS)

In SaaS, users are provided access to applications that are hosted by cloud service vendors. As per the traditional concept, users purchase, download, and then install the required software in their devices. SaaS promotes that their users subscribe to a particular software (monthly or annually) rather than buying it entirely. The software is preinstalled and managed on the service provider-owned systems and users are able to access them over the internet. It reduces the support and maintenance costs, while also allowing users to conserve storage spaces for large applications. Domains like Customer Relationship Management (CRM), finance and accounting, marketing, and business analytics use SaaS for its convenience and efficiency. Google Apps, Dropbox, MailChimp, and Slack are some of the best examples of SaaS that most of us use on a daily basis.

Cloud Bursting

Many organizations often face the challenge of a sudden influx of data traffic either from end users, client sides, or within the organization's private environment itself because of heavy DevOps tasks. These traffic fluctuations can lead to unproductivity or downtime events. Upgrading the private infrastructure and resources to accommodate these bursts might not always turn out to be an affordable and smart investment. In case of CI/CD batch jobs, users will always have the option to fine-tune the configurations to optimize and stretch the implementation over prolonged durations, but this would not be apt for high-priority jobs. Hence, to cope with such unstable traffic scenarios, public clouds should be integrated within the current infrastructure. This will provide a consistently premium experience to clients, customers, and users.

Security in Cloud Infrastructure

While migrating to cloud computing, the major concern of most of the organizations is regarding data security. This is one of the primary reasons many companies hesitate switching over to cloud, as the cloud service vendors might have access to sensitive and business-critical data since services being used will utilize their resources. Some countries also have the jurisdictional authority to dig through such data without any obligation to notify the owning user or organization of the data. A fine example would be the Prism Program by the USA (now considered discontinued).

To prevent such situations and to improve the security of servers, systems, networks, and overall data security, cloud computing service vendors have collaborated with Trusted Computing Group (TCG), a nonprofit organization. They release specifications on a frequent basis providing insights on securing systems, encrypting storage devices, and enhancing network security; this helps in securing systems from malware, rootkits. and ransomware. TCG also shares security instructions for secure portable hard drives, smartphones. and tablets to ensure optimum security over cross-devices for all cloud platforms.

In order to secure the cloud systems, infrastructure, and all data associated with it, cloud computing involves defined controls, processes, policies, and tools working in correlation. These exist to not just secure the data but also to follow regulatory compliances and ensure optimal privacy practices for organizations, along with imposing stringent authentication measures for all users. There are several factors that fall under this wide domain of security in cloud computing.

- Threat prevention, detection, and mitigation

- Access controls

- Data center security

- Redundancy

- Security policies

- Legal compliance

Apart from these, cloud service providers also use some other methods to protect the data of their users like Firewalls, Access Controls, VPN, Data masking (encrypting sensitive data), Threat Intelligence, and Disaster Recovery.

Introduction to Hybrid Cloud Architecture

To reiterate, Hybrid Cloud is usually a combination of public cloud and on-premises infrastructure resources (which may or may not be private cloud). Multiple public clouds, private clouds, and/or on-prem infrastructure could also be combined together to form Hybrid Cloud Architecture. This orchestration among them enables users to migrate data between the public and private clouds with ease and flexibility to satisfy the alternating requirements of organizations.

Hybrid clouds are usually misinterpreted as 'Multicloud,' as both include the integration of multiple cloud environments. In hybrid cloud architecture, multiple clouds of various types are combined (e.g., private-public) whereas multicloud combines multiple clouds of the same type (e.g., public-public or private-private).

Often organizations view the hybrid cloud environments as a temporary setup – for migrations or to handle seasonal traffic spikes. Considering how hybrid clouds might soon be an essential component of modern infrastructural needs, even while developing new systems or upgrading existing ones, the architecture should be strategically planned to extract the perks of multiple infrastructures. It should be quite clear at this point that hybrid cloud uses the best of both worlds, which provides greater benefits over the other two individual cloud models.

- **Scalability**

    Sometimes organizations find it challenging to manage their on-premises infrastructure to meet the demanding needs, especially during an influx of data overflow. This is when public clouds come into the picture to provide aid. You must have gone through the term *cloud bursting* mentioned previously, which facilitates the use of a public cloud when a spike in data traffic overburdens the resources in a private cloud or on-prem infrastructure. This influx varies depending on many factors like geographic locations or regional or international events. To upgrade your on-prem infrastructure to support such temporary requirements would not be a cost-effective option as opting for hybrid cloud architecture and letting public clouds handle these spikes. The same goes for increased storage needs by organizations; public cloud can be used to store uncritical and not frequently accessed data files. Data storage in the public cloud also helps to provide clients or users with secure and easy access to required files.

- **Cost Effectiveness**

    In Hybrid Cloud Architecture, a public cloud enables organizations to fulfill their needs without sustaining permanent expenditure on IT resources and maintenance charges. Users would just have to define suitable configurations, cloud service vendors, and service locations. These resources are scalable, redeployable, and most importantly can be decreased when not required to reduce futile charges. You only pay for the amount and time period of your usage.

- **Data Integration**

    Organizations storing their data in a Hybrid cloud need data synchronization between a public cloud and their on-prem infrastructure/private cloud. Although tricky, with proper tools, configurations and implementations, users can achieve consistent data integration.

Operating Hybrid Clouds

Operation of public and private clouds as a part of hybrid cloud infrastructure is similar to their operation as individual cloud services. However, interconnectivity between the multiple cloud infrastructures is a significant factor, as a lack of it will obstruct proper data alignment over all clouds. Communication between multiple clouds can be established by various methods, as stated below.

VPN

A Virtual Private Network enables clouds to have a private, secure, and encrypted communication through the internet. The encryption of a VPN allows users to connect with other devices and resources regardless of their cloud infrastructure. Using VPN, public and private clouds and/or public and on-prem infrastructure can securely connect while providing authenticated access.

Wide Area Network

Unlike a LAN, WANs connect systems across large distances, which is why it is a preferred mode of connection for many organizations implementing hybrid cloud architecture. WAN provides more reliability compared to a plain vanilla connection over the internet. Even in WAN, connections should still be additionally secured by using a VPN.

API (Application Program Interface)

One of the most important methods for connecting multiple clouds to various applications, platforms, and databases is via an API. Developers use APIs to request other applications or resources to establish a valid connection. An API can be defined as a stack of functions, tools, and routines required to develop an application or software. In a cloud infrastructure, API requests are sent from a system/resource from one cloud network to another in the form of HTTP requests. Based on the communication protocol, they can be sent over VPN, WAN, or public internet.

Apart from these methods, elements akin to containers, virtualization, and software-defined storages (SDS) can also be accumulated into data lakes. Such resources are allocated in environments that are capable of running applications by management software. The resources can be operated on an on-demand basis supported by an authentication service.

Multiple cloud infrastructures can be termed as part of hybrid cloud architecture when all of the related environments are able to connect coherently in an efficient manner. This interconnectivity enables the unification of management, workload, and process orchestration while making hybrid cloud the core element of Edge Computing. The performance of hybrid clouds is directly proportional to reliable connections.

Having mentioned all the advantages of Hybrid Cloud, providing insights on a few limitations should make it a fair game. It is only understandable that while implementing any feature in IT infrastructure, there will always be the existence of pros and cons. Although these could not actually be perceived as cons or disadvantages, they are still important factors worth considering.

To integrate hybrid clouds, there are a few challenges from the design and development standpoint as highlighted below:

- To automate and expedite the software deployments in order to attain quicker marketing with fewer cycle periods.

- Hastening the development under the influence of effective services and APIs.

- Speeding the facilitation of storage and computational resources.

Similarly, following are some prerequisites and limitations from an operational perspective.

- Constant verification of authorization and authentication, along with auditing and compliance of policies over multiple infrastructures.

- Manage complexity by utilizing tools and processes.

- Ensuring to provide visibility over multiple environments.

While glancing at the architectural aspects of hybrid cloud environments, organizations often struggle with following restrictions.

- Software dependencies

- Functioning and latency concerns for system connections

- Exclusively available hardware/OS reliability

- Licensing constraints

Choosing the deployment of workloads in public or private clouds is an acute decision since it will result in the performance and efficacy of hybrid cloud implementation. Deploying an inappropriate workload on a public cloud or vice versa can not only unnecessarily increase the complexity of the infrastructure but also might fail to provide you with the intended results. To amplify the performance, you have to deploy proper applications or workloads in their best-suited cloud environment after intricate analysis. This way you will also get to learn about the key advantages of every environment, which will help you in developing your future cloud strategies.

Cloud First

After switching to cloud environments, one of the most common methods to start using the public cloud aspect of hybrid cloud infrastructure is the approach of *Cloud First*. In this method, any new workloads are instantly deployed on the cloud.

This method does have its advantages like being able to deploy in a fresh and clutterless environment or reducing the amount of data migration to the cloud. However, following this approach will restrict you to extract optimum performance from the hybrid architecture. The new applications or workloads may only be a rather smaller part of your overall infrastructure. Like a spare cog in massive machinery, required - perhaps, necessity - not so much. Leveraging the cloud by the migration of existing elements may derive larger benefits compared to just deploying the entire new workloads to the cloud.

This method also adds complexity to the infrastructure and might also lead to degraded performance and redundancy issues due to potentially unsuitable infrastructure conditions. Thus, it is always recommended to apply the *cloud-first* approach only for selective and suitable workloads by evaluating how to make the best use of cloud environments through a particular deployment.

Migration

While migrating data or applications, users can follow any of the below-mentioned methods, individually or a combination of them as per the requirements.

Lift and Shift

This method includes migrating the workload from a private infrastructure (cloud or on-prem) to a public cloud without altering any crucial changes to the workload. Usually in this method, preset instances (virtual machines) from the current environment are migrated to the cloud computing infrastructure. It is very beneficial to run these virtual instances on cloud computing instead of private infrastructure.

- Virtual instances in cloud environments enable hastening the availability of resources and also prevent the hindering caused while setting up an on-prem infrastructure.

- Users are charged based on their usage of the computing resources without any direct capital expenditure.

- Most of the tasks in cloud environments have an associated automation feature; it lowers the maintenance efforts requiring minimal human intervention, which also helps in cost savings.

- Cloud-native applications can be configured to be auto-scalable, which will allow resources to be utilized when exclusively required.

- Other cloud services can be integrated with the applications, which will provide more convenience and ease of use.

The *lift and shift* approach would be suitable for workloads with a low amount of dependencies on the current infrastructure or applications unable to be restructured like third-party software.

Improve and Move

Sometimes organizations prefer migrating applications to the cloud before upgrading them, which can be viable to certain users. The opposite holds a much greater advantage for most applications. The method of *Improve and Move* involves revamping the already existing application before migrating it to a cloud environment. This approach will refine future deployments and also help users with auto-scaling. Further, your DevOps cycle will also be enhanced as integrating the improved applications with the CI/CD process (which we'll talk about in the next chapter) can speed up the release periods. The *Improve and Move* method would be befitting for applications dependent on private environments that could not be replicated on the cloud, resource-intensive workloads, or applications that do not completely support automated deployments.

Rip and Replace

This method involves the process of eliminating an element and restoring it. Sometimes, upgrading the current workload may not be an affordable solution or even a possibility, mostly because of a new set of requirements or due to outdated resources that will be unsuitable to upgrade. It is always recommended to replace such unrequired or deprecated systems with newer on-prem components or develop cloud-based applications relevant to your cause. This method might be more apt for third-party related applications or workloads that are obsolete or when the related licensing is not cost effective anymore.

Flexibility

Usually, during switching over to cloud infrastructure, the entire task of migrating is carried out considering it as a one-off permanent process. Architects, administrators, and developers design and follow the migration in an orderly manner ensuring the compliance of multiple factors. However, in Hybrid Cloud architecture, the process is not necessarily a permanent one, as you might need the capability to migrate applications, databases, or data across environments as per requirements. To ensure this, there should be flexibility and portability among the infrastructure and workloads.

- While migrating the data or applications across multiple infrastructures, it is advisable to not make any critical changes to it.

- The control and deploying of applications should be accordant over multiple infrastructures.

- The portability of the applications must not hinder their cloud-native compatibility.

Tiered Hybrid Strategy

Almost all applications can be sorted as front end or back end. Applications that users have direct interaction with can be termed as front end. Web UI or Graphical UI of software is a good example of this. Due to this constant engagement with the end users, such applications are performance responsive, leading to periodic deployments of upgraded versions with refined features. Since they are heavily reliant on back-end applications for data and overall functionality, the front-end applications have control over very meager data.

Contrastingly, back-end applications are primarily responsible for handling most of the critical data. Managing data in large volumes while also ensuring their security always remains a bothersome task for developers. Deployments of back-end applications are inconsistently compared to their counterparts, to avoid major breakdowns or compatibility issues.

The concept of a tiered hybrid strategy involves the foremost deployment of front-end applications into the public cloud. The front-end applications are shifted gradually in phases while the back-end applications existing in their current environment stay intact. Keeping the back-end applications in a private infrastructure will help organizations ensure a higher level of data security by protecting all their sensitive data behind their own firewall and security measures.

Benefits of Tiered Hybrid Implementation

Following this strategy offers other benefits too, apart from data security. As mentioned earlier, front ends have a dependency on back-end applications but back ends are not dependent on front ends. Thus shifting and detaching the front-end applications can be not so complicated unlike migration of back-end applications, which would need to be untangled and then reformed back in the cloud environment. Migration of front-end applications is like: less data = less complexity.

In special circumstances when the data handled by back-end applications is contingent on legal or supervisory regulations, it would be better to maintain your data in a private infrastructural environment, on a permanent basis, or as late as figuring out a compliant solution.

Analytical Hybrid Infrastructure

Most organizational data or workloads can be classified as transactional or analytical type. On the one hand, Transactional data includes reciprocal programs from domains of finance, accounting, sales, enterprise resource planning (ERP), and similar programs. Analytical data, on the other hand, deals with programs that are able to modify, analyze, improve, or anticipate data to help make proper decisions.

The concept of analytical hybrid infrastructure involves using these two types of workloads in dually exclusive environments. The core data from the private infrastructure are initially obtained before uploading into a cloud environment, where the data is analytically processed.

Hybrid Edge Cloud Computing

Most users worldwide have uninterrupted, consistent, and high-grade internet service for their personal and professional use. However, there might be unprecedented downtimes or circumstances when this internet connectivity will remain unavailable. Data centers in remote locations, nautical vehicles like aircraft carriers or cruises, small-scale businesses with sporadic connectivity, and in similar scenarios, business or security-sensitive data and transactions might be hampered due to such unreliable network conditions.

This is where the *Edge Hybrid* strategy can prove to be quite beneficial. Using this concept, workloads that are sensitive with respect to time and business aspects can run locally, at the network edge, while the cloud environment is utilized for better purposes. In this *Edge Hybrid* method, the internet connection is a secondary part of the setup, which is mostly used for managerial tasks and synchronizing data between the cloud and the local environment. This strategy has many perks like reduced latency, self-reliability, and reusability of resources.

Modern Hybrid Cloud Architecture

In traditional hybrid clouds, private and public clouds were connected through vast tangled recurring middleware. This intricate labyrinth was a hindrance for migration of applications and data. As technology evolved, so did the definition of hybrid clouds. Unlike traditional hybrid clouds involving the interconnectivity of multiple cloud environments, in modern hybrid clouds, the primary aim is to ensure the flexibility and convenience of the applications.

In this modern pattern of hybrid clouds, applications are developed and deployed in the form of stacked, distinctly, freely connected microservices. It is done by making sure that the very same OS is used throughout all the managed IT landscape and controlled via a consolidated platform (PaaS). Because of this, the ubiquity of the application is inherited to the environments under it. In simple terms, a modern hybrid cloud infrastructure can consist of universal usage of Linux, development and deployment of cloud-native applications, and supervising all components through Kubernetes or Red Hat OpenShift, the most viable orchestration engines.

Utilization of Linux as the sole operating system in all the elements of the hybrid cloud environment synopsizes the entire hardware requirements, while the orchestration engine synopsizes the application requirements. The interconnectivity created due to this facilitates a global computing environment in which applications will have the flexibility of migration irrespective of the environment configurations, that too without using glitchy APIs for compatibility. This linkage also enables developers and administrators to collaborate on their work for DevOps operations.

Security in Hybrid Clouds

As with any other IT architecture, even hybrid clouds can have security loopholes if not installed and configured warily. However, there are a few security obstacles pertaining to hybrid clouds like migrating data, higher entanglement, and overall wider attack range. Nonetheless, even such risks can be mitigated by bolstering the defense through the involvement of multiple environments. The interconnectivity among these environments allows organizations to have the freedom of selecting their preference of data storage depending on their criteria. This also enables the security staff to allocate the unessential storage units for disaster recovery management.

The hybrid cloud security includes three major elements: physical, technical, and administrative. Physical security, as implied from the name, are controls that are used to secure the hardware components. They can be like locks, access restrictions, video surveillance (CCTV), guards, biometric scanners and so on.

The technical element of security can be defined as the controls implemented to safeguard the IT infrastructure and systems. It mostly includes features like system and network authentication, encryption, automation, endpoint security, built-in firewall, control software, orchestration, and more. For example, encryption is encoding the data for confidentiality whether data is at rest or in motion. Automation ensures monitoring and compliance without requiring any human intervention, and also the implementation of security regulations and updating patches. As the technical controls are arguably the most critical aspect of security in hybrid cloud architecture, most of the robust tools for security are based on hardening these controls.

Administrative security controls are events that help to encourage and enlighten users about the importance of cybersecurity, like training, workshops, incident response management, disaster recovery planning, etc. After all, every employee and end user is also responsible for maintaining their end of security controls. In hybrid clouds, as data and resources are conveniently split across multiple cloud environments, users will always have the feature of backups and recovery. Hence creating and following protocols to ensure such security activities are also a part of administrative security controls.

Red Hat Cloud Suite

Red Hat Cloud Suite is designed for provisioning a platform for container-oriented application development, which is created on a cloud infrastructure with immense scalability. Strongly meshed Red Hat technologies are combined in Cloud Suite, which enables users to create cloud infrastructures, cloud-native application development, deployment orchestration, and migration over hybrid cloud architecture.

With the use of Cloud Suite, users gain the capability to shift current workloads to a scalable environment while expediting the latest cloud services related to application development and private cloud. Red Hat Cloud Suite helps operators to deliver services similar to a public cloud, to the development team, all while preserving easier administration and efficiency.

Red Hat Cloud Suite initially uses Red Hat OpenStack Platform or Red Hat Virtualization to build the private cloud element of the core infrastructure. With respect to scalability, either of those options provides highly scalable and secure environments to host the Red Hat OpenShift Container Platform. OCP is responsible for automating the development and deployment of containerized applications. Figure 2-1 illustrates the architecture of Red Hat Cloud Suite in a better way.

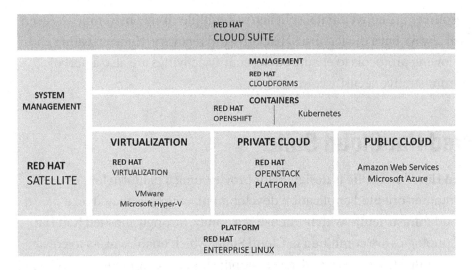

Figure 2-1. *Red Hat Cloud Suite Architecture*

Users will also be able to use the Red Hat Ceph Storage, which is a storage system offering scalability and flexibility along with other features. It is specifically developed to exploit commodity hardware. This helps the OpenStack users with a flawless modular architecture and storage elements integration.

Red Hat CloudForms

CloudForms is the management element of the Cloud Suite architecture. It is responsible for ensuring a constantly seamless management interface, governing over a part, or the entire infrastructure. Users will also be delivered with control, automation, and insight that are required by organizations to overcome the obstacles faced due to virtual infrastructures. CloudForms provides organizations already using cloud environments with better control and visibility, while organizations new into cloud computing are assisted to create and administer a duly maintained virtual infrastructure.

In Red Hat CloudForms different external environments can be handled: managers and providers. CloudForms integrates with a manager or a provider to gather data and execute operations.

- A manager in CloudForms can be described as an exterior management environment, using which multiple resources can be managed. OpenStack is an example of a manager that can manage cloud, storage, network, and infrastructure.

- A provider in CloudForms can be described as an external environment for containers, cloud, or virtualization that is used to manage several VMs or instances present in different hosts. Red Hat Virtualization is an example of a provider that is often utilized to control multiple VMs and hosts.

In Red Hat CloudForms multiple hosts are stacked together to deliver load balancing and high availability, which is known as a cluster. The Clusters Taskbar can be used to handle the tagging and analysis of the clusters.

- In the 'Compute ➤ Infrastructure ➤ Clusters' page, users can view the identified clusters in an enterprise environment.

- To analyse the clusters, users will have to check the cluster clicking through 'Compute ➤ Infrastructure ➤ Clusters ➤ Configuration ➤ Perform SmartState Analysis (The search icon) ➤ OK'.

- This will commence the SmartState Analysis and provide the recent data.

Clusters can also be viewed, compared, and tagged in a similar manner.

Red Hat Virtualization

A premium-level platform for virtualization in servers and systems, Red Hat Virtualization enables the creation, operation, and administration of virtual instances. Developed from RHEL, Red Hat Virtualization includes a Manager (used to handle the VMs and other Virtualization elements), along with a minimum of one Hypervisor (a.k.a. compute nodes or host computers) in order to operate the VMs. Through Red Hat Virtualization Manager, users can perform network configuration, assessment of reports, user management, and also ensure the storage connections. The Virtualization Manager also receives requests from Red Hat CloudForms to integrate its services via API. Red Hat Virtualization will be elaborated further in the next chapters.

Red Hat OpenStack Platform

The OpenStack Platform can be leveraged as a premise for building a public or private IaaS cloud using RHEL. Its main operation is to build and manage VMs, which corresponds to Red Hat Virtualization. However, unlike the latter, Red Hat OpenStack Platform has the capability to divide the virtualization workloads over several controller nodes. Even the OpenStack Platform shares the features of API integration like Virtualization. Red Hat OpenStack will be described in detail in the next chapters.

Red Hat OpenShift Container Platform

Serving as a PaaS, the OpenShift Container Platform makes provisions for application development and deployment in cloud environments. Users can make use of the resources possessing excellent security and scalability, while avoiding the hassle of unnecessary configurations and preventing management and operational expenses. OpenShift Container Platform is discussed in-depth in the upcoming section of this chapter.

Advantages of CloudSuite

Red Hat Cloud Suite offers a user-friendly interface and assembled tools to help with the administration, development, DevOps, networking, operations, and management. Cloud Suite also consists of a management framework over the creation of applications and infrastructure systems. Apart from these, it also provides entire control as well as proper handling of the life cycle with dynamic risk reductions.

Red Hat Cloud Suite is preferred by many developers and DevOps professionals because of accessibility to better computational capabilities and application deployment. It also offers constant integration with multilingual and framework support. Administrators have the ability to control and track such applications and services over a hybrid infrastructure, right until production. Some noteworthy features include the following:

- Modules with full-fledged support and secure integration, all of which help to contribute toward provisioning of open hybrid cloud.

- A sole handy framework for management over the application and infrastructure development layers, in addition to the entire functioning and life-cycle accessibility with dynamic threat prevention.

- Users can improve and upgrade current modules by integrating them with their choice of technology APIs, which ensures no mandatory usage of specific software or tools.

- Cloud Suite also allows you to effortlessly connect additional storage, computational power, networking, and many more cloud tools - not only Red Hat solutions but also open source or ones from different vendors. It can also be utilized on multiple public clouds or even simplistic servers.

Cloud suite provides you with the flexibility to integrate it with your current infrastructure, which allows you to use the favorite features of other third-party or open source applications. This enables you to either connect secondary tools and services to Red Hat Cloud Suite or take advantage of the preexisting features provided by Cloud Suite solutions.

Red Hat Cloud Suite is able to manage multiple cloud solutions ensuring it can provide organizations with all the required tools and technologies for self-sustainability, especially while using hybrid clouds.

- Multiple Virtual Machines (in thousands)

- Storage disks and massive storage arrays

- Single and multiple hypervisors (in hundreds)

- Many virtual as well as physical networks

- On-premises and remote data centers

- Application development and deployment

Orchestration with Red Hat OpenShift

It is of prime importance to present customers with a seamless experience while using an application. After the deployment of an application, ensuring its security, flexibility, scalability, and easy availability are also critical parts of support and service. Thus, many companies are now switching over to containerization platforms like Docker and Kubernetes to fulfill all these requirements. It is necessary to deploy newer applications or even to migrate current applications to the cloud after containerizing them, as organizations need a reliable building platform.

Red Hat OpenShift offers a security-centric and reliable platform for application deployment. Considered as one of the enterprise Kubernetes platform market leaders, Red Hat OpenShift offers automated functioning and efficient development productivity.

OpenShift Container Platform (Red Hat OCP)

Red Hat OpenShift provisions organizations with all the required tools and components for hybrid cloud infrastructure and enterprise containerization. OpenShift consists of advanced and commercial Linux OS, networking for interconnectivity, container runtime, container registry, and authentication/authorization features. All elements are evaluated simultaneously in unison for combined functionality, entirely on a Kubernetes platform comprising each cloud.

Compatibility with Hybrid Cloud

Red Hat OpenShift Container Platform is capable of being used over multiple computing environments including on-prem or private infrastructure and public clouds. This allows it to follow a hybrid cloud pattern for application deployments in the form of an autonomous feature. Apart from Red Hat OpenShift Container Platform, organizations can also utilize the functionality of Red Hat OpenShift Dedicated. It is another OpenShift service that Red Hat is responsible for hosting and managing, which basically provides VPC clusters as its service, through Amazon Web Services, Google Cloud, along with Microsoft Azure Red Hat OpenShift. All these variants enable increased development productivity and ensure portability with application deployment, reliably over the entire hybrid cloud environment.

Red Hat OpenShift yields features like allowing organizations to choose consumption models, either autonomously or Red Hat managed. It provides a solely exclusive console for visibility and management available via *cloud.openshift.com,* along with cohesive metering based on which users are charged.

Figure 2-2 represents the architecture of Red Hat OpenShift Container Platform. RHOCP utilizes Kubernetes and RHEL, integrated with application services, cluster services, and developer services, stacked upon service mesh.

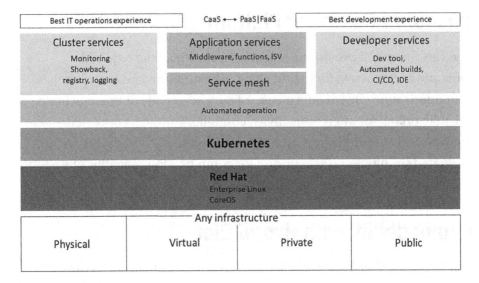

Figure 2-2. *Red Hat OpenShift 4 Architecture*

OpenShift Security

Red Hat is already a world-renowned leading expert in Linux Operating Systems and enterprise-grade open source technologies. Its expertise in containerization technology, especially in Kubernetes development, has been very crucial and innovative. Red Hat OpenShift provides an extensive and consistent secure environment for Kubernetes and it is specifically designed to ensure high security with consistency for OS, applications, and the entire workload development, migration, and deployment process.

Government organizations are very strict about managing their critically classified data. OpenShift is designed to be used in FIPS mode (Federal Information Processing Standards) derived from the RHEL FIPS verified cryptographic libraries. For additional security, users can encrypt the confidential data saved in *etcd*; this is useful to prevent unauthorized data accessibility. OpenShift also enables users in the deployment of clusters to be self-sustained, currently or priorly used VPN/VPC connections along with the usage of private side-load balancing elements.

Distinctive Features

With applications transforming into clusters of independent microservices, controlling the connectivity, security, and compatibility among them can tend to be challenging. OpenShift Mesh Service enables a consistent method for monitoring, controlling, and managing such applications based on microservices.

To tackle the challenges related to scalability, Red Hat OpenShift Serverless model provisions applications to utilize the computational resources and perform automated scalability depending on the usage. Due to this, the burdening computational power requirement and development maintenance are also reduced. Serverless applications can be developed, processed, and deployed, which can be scaled higher or lower up to zero as per the demands, all through OpenShift Serverless.

Red Hat OpenShift Pipeline enables the entire delivery pipeline to be managed by the development team, along with administering plug-ins and accessibility, as there is no CI/CD server to look after. This module allows every part of the CI/CD process to be run in an isolated container, which provides individual scalability for each container and its respective process. All of this provides an efficient and modernized user experience via the CLIs, IDEs, and OpenShift console.

Besides these capabilities, Red Hat OpenShift provides many useful features and benefits:

- High Scalability

- Persistent Storage

- Portability of containers

- Multicluster Federation

- Self-Sustainability

- Automated DevOps Cycle

- Convenient User Interface

- Deployment from source code to container images

- Automated installations and updates

- Sturdy Environment

Kubernetes

Unlike traditional application development, modern applications are created and deployed through containers that use container images to run. To incorporate these containers with scalability, the demand for a secure, portable, and versatile distribution system should be met. Hailed by the community as the best available system for orchestrating containers, Kubernetes (K8s) bridges this gap between such requirements and innovation.

An open source system for container orchestration, Kubernetes enables automation for processes including scalability of applications, its deployment, and also container management. The primary functions of Kubernetes can be explained as the following:

- To process the containerized applications, beginning with one or multiple worker nodes.

- Management of container deployments, through one or multiple master nodes.

- Stack multiple containers within the same deployed unit using pods, which envelop containers in a sole deployment system and deliver additional metadata of the containers.

- Building distinctive assets like a group of pods and accessibility policy representing the services. The said policy enables containers to establish a connection with the required services, whether or not they possess the respective IP addresses of those services. To determine the number of Pod Replicas needed to run simultaneously, Replication Controllers are utilized. This feature can be used to perform automated scalability for the applications to ensure it stays adaptive toward the fluctuating demands.

Because of such productive features, a growing amount of organizations are now implementing Kubernetes for their private on-prem and/or cloud environment. Although initially developed by Google and now maintained by the Cloud Native Computing Foundation, this open source system offers users the flexibility to integrate it with various other elements and technologies, which further widens the usability domain.

Kubernetes takes care of organizing computer clusters that are extremely available and are interconnected to operate as a single entity. Using Kubernetes, containerized applications can be deployed into a cluster without linking them specifically to any machine. There are two primary resources in a Kubernetes cluster:

- Master

  The master controls the cluster by organizing tasks in the cluster that include scheduling applications, maintaining the preferred application state, application scalability, and delivering the latest updates.

- Nodes

  Nodes can be described as physical systems or VMs serving as worker machines in a Kubernetes cluster. Every node comprises an agent known as a Kubelet that handles the node and its communication with the Kubernetes master. Tools like rkt or docker are also included in the node, to control the container operations.

After the application deployment on Kubernetes, the master receives instructions to run the application containers. Based on that, the containers are scheduled to be run on the nodes of the cluster. The Kubernetes API is used for communication between the master and nodes. The API can also be utilized by end users for cluster interaction.

The Kubernetes clusters are deployable on physical systems as well as VMs. Minikube is used for Kubernetes development. It is a form of lightweight Kubernetes than can be used to create a VM on the local host while a basic cluster with a single node is deployed. General bootstrapping operations for clusters like start, status, stop, and delete are enabled through the Minikube CLI.

After the installation of Minikube, the following commands can be used for basic operations.

To check the minikube version:

```
minikube version
```

To start the minikube:

```
minikube start
```

The kubectl CLI can be used for Kubernetes interaction.
To verify the cluster details:

```
kubectl cluster-info
```

To display the cluster nodes:

```
kubectl get nodes
```

To build an application on Kubernetes, the name of the deployment and the location of the application image (repo url) need to be mentioned.

```
kubectl create deployment kubernetes-chadwick --image=app.io/
repo/xyz/kubernetes-chadwick:v1
```

To view the deployment list, use:

```
kubectl get deployments
```

Use the following command to create a proxy through which communications can be rerouted to the private network across the cluster. Pressing Ctrl+C will terminate the created proxy.

```
kubectl proxy
```

As per the pod name, default endpoints for every pod is created by the API server. To view the pod name, use:

```
export POD_NAME=$(kubectl get pods -o go-template --template
'{{range .items}}{{.metadata.name}}{{"\n"}}{{end}}') echo Name
of the Pod: $POD_NAME
```

To view current pods, use:

```
kubectl get pods
```

To view details regarding the pods, use:

```
kubectl describe pods
```

To view the running services in the cluster, use:

```
kubectl get services
```

The default service kubernetes is generated after the cluster initiation by minikube. In order to generate a new service and connect with global traffic, use the following command:

```
kubectl expose deployment/kubernetes-chadwick --type=
"NodePort" --port 8080
```

Use the following command to create an environment variable with the assigned node port value:

```
export NODE_PORT=$(kubectl get services/kubernetes-chadwick -o
go-template='{{(index .spec.ports 0).nodePort}}')
echo NODE_PORT=$NODE_PORT
```

These commands provide a basic overview of Kubernetes operations, and for an in-depth understanding of its functioning you can refer to the documentation of Kubernetes.

Instead of using the traditional application deployment method, organizations prefer adopting the modern way of deploying applications in the form of containers. In this process of virtualization, applications are deployed without being required to launch a complete VM dedicated for every application. Many individually segregated services or applications are processed on a sole host and leverage the resources of the same OS kernel. In the traditional deployment method, to make an application work efficiently, all of its dependencies were also required to be installed in the same OS along with the application itself. In the case of containerized applications, all the required dependencies are provided and installed alongside the application in the container itself.

Linux operating systems without kernels are used within the containers. Having their own networking, file systems, process tables, namespaces, and cgroups, the containers also have the flexibility and independence to utilize and integrate the resources of the host OS, whenever required. Use of Linux allows the containers to reap the benefits associated with the open source technology. Due to the usage of dedicated OS for every container, applications with contrasting dependency needs can be deployed on the same host. Every container is made to self-sustain its required programs and services while handling its own components like the file system and networking, preventing multiple containers from sharing such resources. All of these are pre-declared in the container images, using which the containers are created and run.

In Red Hat OpenShift Container Platform, RHCOS (Red Hat Enterprise Linux CoreOS) is used, which is a next-gen container OS technology. All cluster systems have RHCOS running as their main functioning OS, as it is the best combination of Red Hat Atomic Host OS and CoreOS. RHCOS is exclusively developed to run containerized applications through the Red Hat OCP while operating with better and improvised programs; this enables faster and smooth installations and streamlined updating. Red Hat Core OS uses some specific utilities for efficient functioning:

- The Red Hat OSP wields Ignition for its initial boot-up configuration of the system, to set up and get the systems running.

- In order to provide a seamless and enhanced Kubernetes performance, CRI-O (Container Runtime Interface for Kubernetes) is utilized, which is directly integrated with the OS. CRI-O enables activities like starting, terminating, restarting, or enabling the containers. It is a complete replacement for the DCE (Docker Container Engine), a previously used tool in RHOCP 3.

- The Kubernetes main node agent, Kubelet, is used, which enables the activating and assessing of the containers.

The default use of RHCOS in all control plane systems of OCP provides better efficiency than previous technologies. Users can also use RHEL as the primary OS for computational systems, also referred to as worker machines. Usage of RHEL in worker machines requires additional maintenance of the systems, compared to RHCOS used in all the cluster machines.

OCP Life Cycle

The life cycle of Red Hat OpenShift container includes the following elements:

- Building an OCP cluster

- Cluster management

- Application development and deployment

- Application scalability

The Red Hat OpenShift Container Platform is represented in Figure 2-3. The cluster installer manages the OpenShift cluster creation, and containerized applications are developed and deployed through the application developer, while the cluster manager is responsible for the management of the OpenShift clusters.

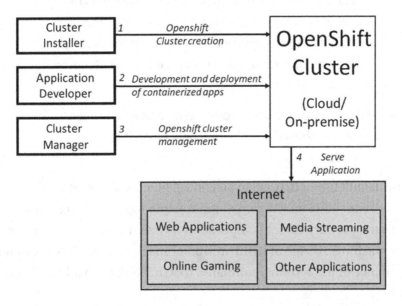

Figure 2-3. *Illustration of Red Hat OpenShift Container Platform*

OCP Installation

The Red Hat OpenShift Container Platform provides a flexible installation procedure and preference. Using the installation software, a cluster can either be deployed on a custom-provisioned and cluster-maintained infrastructure or on a private infrastructure, as per the convenience of the user.

There are two primary types of OCP clusters: installer-provisioned infrastructure and user-provisioned infrastructure. Whichever cluster type is chosen, users will find a few common attributes:

- Infrastructure with high availability, ensuring zero failure points (by default).

- Time and type of update patching are entirely controllable by the administrators.

Both types of clusters can be deployed using the single installation program. The primary files created by the installation program include the master and worker systems, as well as the bootstrap Ignition config files. Using these three assets and infrastructure with proper configuration, an OCP cluster can be initiated.

A stack of multiple dependencies and targets are utilized by the OCP installation program to handle installing the clusters. The installation program is responsible for fulfilling a target set, each of which has its own dependencies. As targets manage their self-dependencies, more targets can be parallelly attained. The eventual outcome is supposed to be a cluster execution. To fulfill the dependency requirements, the installation program evaluates and makes use of current elements, rather than using commands for their recreation.

Figure 2-4 depicts a subunit of an installation target and dependencies.

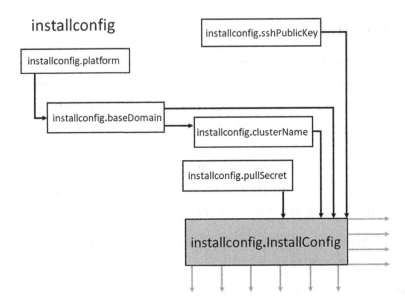

Figure 2-4. Red Hat OpenShift Container Platform targets and dependencies

Post-installation, RHCOS is used as the primary OS for every cluster. With RHEL features embedded into it and SELinux enabled, RHCOS provides optimum security. It consists of the Kubernetes node agent and kubelet along with the Kubernetes optimized CRI-O (Container Runtime Interface-Open Container Initiative) container runtime.

Installation Procedure

Red Hat OCP operates with a makeshift bootstrap system through the startup configuration providing needed data to the control plane, as every machine in the cluster needs data about the cluster while being equipped. The Ignition config file describing the creation of the cluster is responsible for booting up the system. The master machines that are key for the control plane are created by the bootstrap system. This then leads to the master machines creating the computational machines, better known as worker machines or worker nodes. Figure 2-5 depicts this installation process.

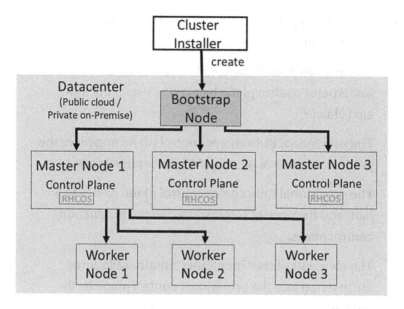

Figure 2-5. *Creation of the Bootstrap, Master, and Worker Machines*

Post the cluster machines initialization, the bootstrap machine is dismantled as it is no longer required. To launch the cluster, the bootstrap process is exploited by all the clusters. However, in case of a user-provisioned infrastructure, the user is responsible for manually finishing most of the steps.

The below-mentioned actions are required to bootstrap a cluster:

- Post the booting of the bootstrap machine, it commences the hosting of the remote resources that are needed for the booting of the master machines. In case the infrastructure is custom provisioned, the process will need manual interference.

- To conclude the booting, the remote resources are procured from the bootstrap machine by the master machines. In case the infrastructure is custom provisioned, the process will need manual interference.

- The bootstrap machine is used by the master machines to create an etcd cluster.

- The bootstrap machine begins a provisional Kubernetes control plane by making use of the new etcd cluster.

- The provisional Kubernetes control plane organizes the production control plane to the master machines.

- The provisional Kubernetes control plane comes to a halt, and the control is transferred to the production control plane.

- The elements of the OpenShift Container Platform are inserted into the provisional control plane by the bootstrap machine.

- Later, the operation of the bootstrap machine is ceased by the installation program. In case the infrastructure is custom provisioned, the process will need manual interference.

- The control plane initiates and configures the worker nodes.

- Later, the control nodes manage the installation of the additional services, featured as a set of Operators.

This bootstrapping process leads to a completely functional OpenShift Container Platform cluster. The residual elements are then downloaded and configured, which are required for the routine activities, like the formation of worker machines in compatible environments.

CHAPTER 3

Security in DevOps and Automation

An amalgamation of the words "Development" and "Operations," the term "DevOps" was coined by *Patrick Debois* in 2009. It can be defined as a harmonized blend of practices, technologies, culture, and mindset to enable automation and integration of the activities among application development and IT operations teams so as to amplify the building, testing, and deployment processes more efficiently. Once used as a generic term, now DevOps has evolved into an umbrella domain consisting of operations, tools, and culture that shrinks the application development life cycle, through quicker feedback loops that provide functionality, features, and upgrades on a consistent basis.

In traditional IT methods, the development and operations teams operated as silos. The newer DevOps model requires both teams to function in unison, administering the complete software life cycle from development to testing and later to deployment. DevOps originated from two of its prior forerunners. We'll cover those first and then get into DevSecOps, a combination of "development," "security," and "operations."

Categories of DevOps

The culture of a DevOps model entails many subcategories that are virtually common in most organizations.

© Rithik Chatterjee 2021
R. Chatterjee, *Red Hat and IT Security*,
https://doi.org/10.1007/978-1-4842-6434-8_3

Automation

The entire process of DevOps has a major dependency on automation, for which various tools are essential. These tools can be from third-party vendors, or built-in functionality of a service provider, proprietary or open source. It is all up to the requirements and financial leeway provided to the teams. This use of tools is commonly referred to as *Toolchain* in DevOps, in which tools and technologies are used for development, deployment, and maintenance of applications, as per the Agile Manifesto. DevOps is largely dependent on *Toolchain* for simplified automation of the end-user application development and deployment phases.

Continuous Integration (CI)

As DevOps is derived from agile development, features like continuous integration have sustained a prime role even in this culture. In continuous integration (CI), the updates for source code by all the individuals of a development team are merged into the master branch. This process of constant merging of the code versions helps developers to avoid the codes from their local systems to deviate from the original source code, which fends off troublesome merge conflicts.

Continuous Testing (CT)

The continuous testing process can be defined as the execution of tests in an automated manner, incorporated in the software development and delivery life cycle, so as to keep receiving valuable feedback based on it. The process involves a repetitive cycle of software testing while automating the process. The objective of continuous testing is to carry out testing in the early stages and to do it often. This process quickens the software delivery cycle while improving the code quality and also assessing the risk coverage for organizations. The continuous feedback loop enables a better and efficient agile process. Continuous testing is also helpful to eliminate the testing constrictions by using services that make it easier to create virtualized testing environments, which possess the flexibility for upgrading, sharing, and deployment processes. Due to this, the maintenance and provisioning costs also decrease.

Agile Development

DevOps is often considered to be an evolutionary process derived from agile application development. It consists of different techniques and practices revolving around the concept of an iterative development procedure, in which specifications and solutions are transformed by cooperative efforts amid independent and multifunctional teams. The agile application development stipulates a collaborative process involving the development and operations team, clients/customers, and at times even the QA team. It is a vital aspect to ensure seamless service delivery and deployment along with interactive systems and applications, which is a determining factor for the USP of a product or service, offered to the users. Hence such concerns are highly prioritized to improve the product and development life cycle. In hindsight, DevOps may just seem like an extension of the principles from the Agile Manifesto, a more refined and coherent version.

Enterprise Systems Management (ESM)

A large chunk of technologists associated with the initial phases of DevOps consisted of system administrators. With their expertise in operations, they instituted the crucial best practices from ESM, which comprised handling the configurations, automation, toolchain strategy, and monitoring.

Continuous Delivery vs. Continuous Deployment

In the DevOps cycle, CD can stand for either of two terms: Continuous Delivery or Continuous Deployment. Although both of the concepts have similarities between them, there is also the presence of a substantial difference that could prove to have a vital impact on a production environment.

Continuous Delivery (CD)

Continuous delivery can be considered as an extended part of CI, to ensure that the new software releases are delivered to the clients and users in a swift, reliable, and continual method. After automating CI and CT, by enabling automation with the release process, a software can be delivered without requiring constant changes. Theoretically, with continuous delivery, new releases for software can be scheduled as per the requirements, like weekly, monthly, or quarterly. However, it is recommended to always plan and roll out releases at the earliest so as to achieve buffer time for potential troubleshooting issues.

Continuous Deployment (CD)

In continuous deployment, all changes that pass the individual phases of the DevOps pipeline are released in the production environment. Requiring absolutely minimal human intervention in the entire process, the only thing that will prevent the deployment of a new modification/release is a failed test result. Continuous deployment reduces the burden on the development, testing, and operations teams because of quick and efficient deployments. In simpler terms, it can be stated that continuous deployment is almost like continuous delivery, barring the feature of automated production releases. The main and standout difference is that in continuous delivery, the teams are responsible for deciding the release date and process, whereas, in continuous deployment, software versions are released through an automated deployment workflow.

Continuous Monitoring

An integral part of the management phase of the production pipeline, continuous monitoring represents the tools and processes used to monitor the various aspects of the DevOps life cycle. This includes the monitoring of system health, availability, performance, functioning, and other aspects as well. Built on the concept of CI/CD, the process of continuous monitoring is usually executed using APM (Application Performance Management) solutions. These have astute abilities to analyze, monitor, provide stability, and even manage the services and applications across multiple environments. APMs also help to quickly assess the underlying causes of issues and impede potential malfunctions or system downtimes. Similar to testing, continuous monitoring also begins in development. Experts believe that there should, in fact, be two forms of monitoring in place for DevOps, monitoring for application performance and also server monitoring, each helping in a different way to enrich the ultimate user experience.

Figure 3-1 depicts the DevOps life cycle, which is a continuous process and hence, is often represented by the infinity symbol portraying the unending life cycle and all its associated processes.

Figure 3-1. *DevOps Life Cycle*

Benefits of DevOps

There are several benefits of incorporating DevOps in a general software development life cycle (SDLC).

Scalability

With automated scalable cloud infrastructures, even development processes need to adapt and implement a consistent automated production pipeline. All of the cloud services can be managed in a very efficient way with DevOps, like IaaS enables users to manage multiple environments like development, testing, and production, iteratively and effectively. DevOps helps with the scalability of modern private, public, or hybrid infrastructures, being able to process alternating and complex system changes.

Speed

DevOps accelerates the entire process from application development to testing and later to the release of the product/software. New features and modifications are rolled out much earlier than usual through an automated implementation of CT and CI/CD. The DevOps pipeline is always designed in such a way to scan for any bugs, issues, or new updates. This reduces the time required for assessments and with continuous monitoring, such tasks take a significantly lower time frame, thus increasing the overall speed, be it for new releases or troubleshooting issues. Additionally, by using *Value Stream Mapping,* users are able to assess congestion and unnecessary processes in the production cycle. Fixing them would also result in higher speed in productivity and deployments.

Innovation

Often overlooked in many businesses, the factor of innovation is also crucial for the betterment of any product. Courtesy of increased speed and stability, the development team can utilize the saved time and efforts into focusing on PoC (Proof of Concept)-based experimentations by trying out extra features that can make the product even better and stand out from its competitors. Such trials and errors will prove to be useful to determine the feasibility of various ideas and strategies.

Agility

A DevOps model enables an organization to have flexibility in its workflow, by acquiring the capability to manage *cloud bursts* or resource overheads. This helps organizations gain a better understanding of their customer's usage patterns and statistics for different applications and environments. Adopting DevOps also helps to adapt smoothly to change management by minimizing outages. It may always be arguable whether implementing a DevOps model in a software development cycle results in agility or is it the other way around. Regardless, developing an agile mindset, culture, operations, and technologies are the best moves forward in the current IT landscape.

Qualitative Growth

DevOps can undoubtedly increase the quality of a software or product through its functionality in the production pipeline. Traditional software testing methods are scrapped and new, better systems are used instead. Integrating and testing vital elements all over the software development life cycle are made easier with a systematic and distributed workflow. An application can be upgraded with new features that may only result from such coherent techniques.

Reliability

Following a DevOps approach also increases the reliability of services and applications. It can be referred to as the means by which a system can perform smoothly, consistently, and provide uninterrupted services. Adopting a DevOps model enhances the availability of services and interconnectivity among them, essential for every production life cycle.

Cost-Effective

DevOps also helps with cost-effectiveness, from a business perspective like the following:

- System/Network outage costs
- Software/Application/Product release costs
- Maintenance and productivity costs

Evolution of DevSecOps

As implied from the name itself, DevSecOps stands for Development, Security, and Operations. Many organizations implementing DevOps do so with a notion to abridge the siloed teams and automate the entire SDLC so as to be able to release their products with better speed and stability. Amid all this, more often than not security takes a hit and is often ignored as a compromisable factor. With growing cybersecurity threats looming over IT technologies, organizations and users should always stay wary of and prioritize security alongside the other aspects.

DevSecOps can be considered as an upgrade over the normal DevOps initiative. It is usually associated with the tagline of *Shift Left* security, which refers to shifting the security phase at the earliest possible point in an SDLC, since troubleshooting or intercepting security issues at the latter end can be more tedious and challenging. One of the prime principles while implementing DevSecOps is striving to place quality adjacent to the source by ensuring higher security measures. What this means is, the DevSecOps model emphasizes incorporating high-grade security within the SDLC and the applications as well, rather than affixing it as an additional patchwork.

DevSecOps also enables automating certain security checkpoints to prevent workflow deceleration of the DevOps cycle. This can include something as simple as proper selection of security tools and enabling embedded security features in preexisting applications and technologies. Having said that, a definitive DevSecOps framework extends beyond the use of mere tools, as a cultural change along with elaborate security implementation is more essential.

To provide a better picture, you can assume a hypothetical scenario, wherein cyber attackers were somehow able to penetrate the first wall of defense, after which they executed a malware or spyware into your application during the development process. Modern malware is re-engineered to stay under the radar, completely undetected even from developers and security tools that are unable to trace their signatures. This planted malware goes undetected and gets distributed worldwide through your application, affecting millions of people, not to mention the catastrophic damage caused to the competency and reputation of your organization. Such situations might be improbable but surely not impossible, as this was just an example out of countless similar possibilities where security can be compromised unless worked on.

DevSecOps is about implementing security as a built-in component instead of an element encompassing the applications, data, or environment. Like determining the risk tolerance and analyzing the associated risks and benefits, it is a decent implementation of this framework. Similarly figuring out the required security controls, automation for an application, among other factors, can help create a detailed blueprint to execute the security aspects of this model. Threat modeling routines can be one of the most effective methods to explore security bugs and vulnerabilities of applications. The discovered flaws can be amended with the required security changes.

Built-in security within the SDLC instead of an added layer of security enables DevOps to collaborate with security experts to extract the core perk of agile techniques: '*Together as a team - without short-circuiting the goal of creating secure code*'.

As per an EMA report of 2017, the two most advantageous highlights of SecOps are these: an improved ROI in the preexisting IT security environment and an enhanced operational proficiency over security and other IT environments as well.

There are a few more benefits reaped from the implementation of a DevSecOps framework:

- Quick responsiveness to requirements and changes.

- Accelerated and agile performance by the security team.

- Increased options for automation-oriented builds and QA testing.

- Prior assessments of vulnerabilities and threats in the entire SDLC including the code.

- Qualitative inter-team alliance.

A combined effort to transform the cultural mindset along with the technical aspects play a major role in establishing a well-functioning DevSecOps model. It also enables organizations to tackle the threats in security much more efficiently on a real-time basis. Instead of perceiving the security as an agility barrier liability, it should be regarded as a crucial asset that can help avoid stagnation. For instance, analyzing and detecting a defective application that will be unable to scale when in a cloud environment could help save precious time, efforts, computing resources, and expenditure too. Cloud environments demand high-scale embedded security configurations to ensure application scalability. Constant and consistent threat modeling with the handling of system builds are required to sufficiently meet the needs of emerging technologically oriented organizations.

The six most vital elements of the DevSecOps framework can be described as these:

- Code Analysis

  Code is delivered in smaller parts to facilitate faster detection of security vulnerabilities.

- Change Management

  Pace and productivity rise due to approving submission for changes by all valid users, and later ascertain the viability of each change.

- Compliance Monitoring

  All operations must be constantly following all the policies and guidelines as per the standard regulations like GDPR and PCI compliance. This prevents the occurrence of noncompliance flags even during impromptu audits.

- Threat Analysis

  Detecting, identifying, and analyzing latent transpiring threats within each part of the code and its following updates to be able to develop swift responsiveness.

- Vulnerability Assessment

  Analyzing the code for identification of concealed vulnerabilities, be it in the form of errors or possible backdoors. Post that, carry analysis over such patch fixes and their usability timeline.

- Security Training

  Conduct training sessions or workshops to enlighten IT professionals, especially developers, testers, and administrators, over the compliance of cybersecurity measures and guidelines for set security routines.

The DevSecOps model is considered an extension of the preexisting DevOps model, so security modules and processes are blended with the DevOps model. For instance, it can be compared to a software, where DevSecOps is not a brand new software, but instead just an updated version of the previous DevOps Software. Figure 3-2 depicts the same.

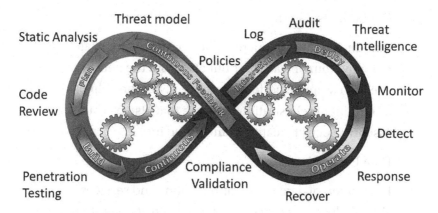

Figure 3-2. *DevSecOps Life Cycle*

The DevSecOps framework can be implemented not only for the application being developed but also for the CI/CD process, computing environment, infrastructure, data, and also the end users.

DevSecOps in Environment and Data Security

- Privilege Standardization

  There should be standardization and automation in place for the computing environment. Every service must possess only the bare essential security privilege required for its proper functioning, so as to reduce unauthorized accesses.

- Strict Authentication

  Stringent centralization of user identification and access management processes are required to enable the security of microservices, by ensuring multi-point authentication.

- Container Isolation

    Containers that run microservices must be segregated
    not only from one another but also from the network
    itself. This can be perfectly achieved with the help of
    a container orchestration platform that also has other
    essential security features embedded into it.

- Data Encryption

    Encryption of data within applications and services
    should always be provisioned. Data at rest, in motion,
    and data currently being used, all should be equally
    encrypted and secured to avoid any potential
    exposures for attackers to explore.

- Secure API Support

    Integrated API gateways should always provide users
    with ample security to prevent any data compromise.
    APIs that are secured improve authorization
    capabilities. Decreasing the use of insecure APIs will
    also help with routing visibility and allow organizations
    to avert attack areas.

DevSecOps in CI/CD Pipeline

- Container Security

    Security scanners for containers should be integrated.
    This is supposed to be inclusive of the container adding
    a process to the registry.

- Scanning and Testing

  Testing of security in the CI process should be automated
  by executing security tools for static analysis as a build
  component. Prefabricated container images must also be
  scanned for security threats or vulnerabilities since even
  those are inherited by the eventual code derived from
  the compromised container.

- Automated Testing

  The acceptance test procedure must include automated
  security tests by automating authenticated verifications,
  tests for input validations, and authorization attributes.

- Automated Updates

  Update rollouts, especially ones to patch known
  security vulnerabilities (verified through the CVE
  database) must be automated as much as possible. The
  process, done via the DevOps pipeline, is supposed to
  extinguish the necessity of an administrator logging
  in the production systems, along with the generation
  of change logs that are well-documented and can be
  traced back.

- Compliance Management

  The process of managing the service and system
  configurations should also be automated. This
  will ensure the compliance of security standards
  and regulations and avoidance of manual faults.
  Additionally, auditing, rectifications, and amendments
  can also be automated in a similar manner to enhance
  the overall security outlook.

Infrastructure as Code and Security as Code

Infrastructure as Code (IaC)

IaC can be described as the procedure to manage and provision system data centers via definition files that are in machine-readable format instead of specifying the configurations for the physical hardware or through some synergistic applications. In layman's terms, IaC can be interpreted as handling and controlling the IT infrastructure with the help of configuration files. It utilizes a high-grade expository programming language, which is used for automating the implementation of infrastructure environments and its elements. The process of automation extinguishes the requirement of any manual intervention to configure, control, and secure the servers, systems, operating systems, storages, database links, and other components of the infrastructure, whenever the need arises for any process in the SDLC.

Many organizations deploy multiple applications on a consistent basis, which involves frequent spin-ups, disintegration, and scaling of infrastructure components depending on the development and user requirements. This makes it an absolute necessity for organizations to embrace the infrastructure automation provided by IaC, so as to efficiently handle capital expenditure, enhance the speed of production workflow, and minimize security vulnerabilities. This, in turn, will also lead to increased business opportunities while acquiring a competitive edge in the market.

Modern DevSecOps frameworks implement IaC as one of its imperative elements to strengthen the SDLC. This allows the DevOps/DevSecOps team to quickly build, deploy, and version infrastructure similar to that of source code versioning. Due to this, tracking and maintaining records of each version becomes easy, which helps prevent disparities and repetitive issues.

Although cloud-native application development and virtualization reduces the issue of manually managing the hardware that allows the development team to create and arrange servers, systems, and containers virtually as per the requirements. However, this process still consists of building virtualized environments or components that can be a tedious and intrusive task, sidetracking the development team from programming, and they need to keep repeating this process multiple times for fresh deployments. Due to this, it becomes difficult to keep track of all the modifications made to the environment to avoid disparities that would affect the releases.

One of the key concepts of IaC is *Idempotence*. In this feature, after executing the command for deployment, the intended environment will always be set up in the exact configuration, irrespective of the initial state of the environment. *Idempotence* can be implemented by an automated configuration of the current environment or by disposing of the current environment and then rebuilding a new one from scratch.

As a result, with respect to IaC, modifications are made to the description of the environment while versioning the configuration model. This is usually done in properly recorded code formats like JSON. Execution of the model by the deployment pipeline ensures a seamless configuration of the target environments. In case any changes are to be made, it is done so by editing the source rather than the target.

IaC offers many benefits to users apart from a systemized infrastructure with version control.

- **Reduced *Configuration Drift***

    Whenever improvised configurations are made through alterations or upgraded releases, it may cause a discrepant workflow; such an event is referred to as *configuration drift*. This process can cause snags in releases, security threats, and potential standard and regulation compliance challenges during development.

Implementing IaC eliminates this *configuration drift* by enabling developers to provide the same infrastructure every time.

- **Increased Production Timeline**

  The entire process of building the infrastructure for the SDLC process is drastically hastened because of the automated features provided by IaC. It can compile and maintain documentation systematically. This enables the automation associated with the legacy infrastructure that is usually controlled by arduous and intensive processes.

- **Rapid & Coherent Development**

  IaC has the ability to pace each process of the SDLC through simplification of provisioning and verifying the consistency of the environment and infrastructure. This enables the development team to handle swift sandbox provisioning and a CI/CD pipeline. Then QA can handle the fast provisioning of test environments with full fidelity. The operation team can manage the similarly swift infrastructure provisioning for security and a friendly testing experience. After the code has successfully cleared the testing, both the production environment and the application can be released altogether.

- **Defensive Measure against *churn***

  In order to increase the productivity of an organization, they will hand over the process of provisioning to a select few engineers or IT professionals. In case any such specialists leave the organization, the processes

she/he was responsible for, could not be replicated by
other employees. This would leave the process to be
rebuilt, whereas IaC will enable organizations to keep
the provisional intelligence to themselves instead of
specific individuals.

- **Reduced Expenditure and Better ROI**

  Apart from minimizing the efforts, time, and
  characteristic skills that are required to build and
  scale the environments, IaC also allows organizations
  to exploit the perks of the consumption-oriented
  cost structure of cloud computing. It also helps the
  development team to focus more of their time on
  programming while discovering new ingenious
  applications and services.

While choosing to implement IaC, organizations need to choose
between the two types of IaC: *mutable* and *immutable* infrastructure.
Depending on individual needs and functionality, the preferred selection
will reap benefits in different ways.

Mutable Infrastructure can be described as an infrastructure that is
feasible to be altered even post its initial installation. As the term 'mutable'
states, the infrastructure can be mutated if desired or as per the changing
needs. This gives developers the required adaptability to create improvised
server configurations so as to resemble the application and development
demands or even as a resolution for an extreme security problem. Having
said that, this feature impairs one of the primary perks of IaC, that is, the
capability to sustain consistency among the releases or various versions,
thus making the version tracking of the infrastructure very challenging.

Many organizations prefer *immutable infrastructure* to preserve that
consistent behavior of IaC, which precedes all other requirements. As
opposed to its counterpart, *immutable infrastructure* cannot be altered in

any way after its initial installation. If any situation arises to make some changes to the *immutable infrastructure,* it has to be completely reinstalled with a fresh infrastructure. Since creating new infrastructure in the cloud is easier and takes only a matter of minutes especially with IaC, *immutable infrastructure* is actually more practical and conceivable than it seems.

Organizations have to also select between the two different types of approaches while implementing the automation associated with IaC.

The *imperative approach,* which is also referred to as the *procedural approach*, enables users to create scripts for automation that perform the infrastructure provisioning in individual phases, one after the other. Although this can prove to be tedious as infrastructures are scaled up, it can also be convenient and easy for the current administration team to operate and utilize the configuration scripts that are predominantly used.

The *declarative approach* is better known as the *functional approach* in many organizations, wherein the required eventual infrastructure setup is defined and the IaC program manages the task. They include creating virtualized servers or containers, application installations and configurations, processing system and application dependencies, interconnectivity, and version control. The primary disadvantage of this method is that it usually needs a proficient administrator to handle and set up the entire process, as such admins have expertise in solutions they prefer to work on.

Using either of these approaches can be loosely compared to using an automated electric car vs. using a manual muscle car. With the automated electric car, many functions, like the ABS or traction control system, are automated and handled by the AI of the car software, leaving only technical experts to figure out how these systems actually operate. In the case of a muscle car, experienced professional drivers are well versed with pushing such a powerful beast to its limits and to efficiently control its every behavior. One is best for drag racing while the other is most suitable for a cross-country drive. The same goes for both the IaC approaches mentioned above.

Security as Code (SaC)

During software development, equal importance is given to security while executing each phase of the SDLC workflow. This means integrating security tools, practices, and the mindset deep within the core of the culture and DevOps pipeline. Execution of security as part of the original source code can be termed *security as code.* It is actually merging security in the earlier phases of the life cycle, from development to DevOps. This will enable resolving issues identified as part of the code, which can be fixed with security patches and updates.

SaC makes use of continuous delivery as one of its core components and automation engines for administering the overall security. As mentioned earlier, continuous delivery is the SDLC phase of rendering and making configurations to the testing environments in order to accord with the production requirements in an automated manner. The process of continuous delivery ensures that the software or any modifications made to it extends to the end user/client in a definitive way. SaC is an additional security skin over the existing workflow, especially when it comes to the DevOps pipeline.

While infusing SaC into your production environment, you need to be aware of the two primary types of threats faced at the coding level:

- Buffer Overflow

- Code Injection

It is important to understand these threats, what they are, and how they function, before enforcing a defensive strategy against them.

Buffer Overflow

A program or code contains multiple variables, and when those are used, our system stores those variables in a temporary memory known as a buffer. Whenever data surpassing the limits of this buffer are attempted to be accessed, buffer overflow transpires. Buffer overflow attacks can lead the attackers to compromise the system, thieve, or contaminate the data. Generally, there are two types of buffer overflow attacks as mentioned below.

- **Stack Buffer Overflow**

  A data structure in which data can be appended or erased only through the top in a stack. As stack variables are used in a code, the system stores those variables within the stack. When a code writes to a temporary memory address, which is further the aimed memory of the call stack, a stack buffer overflow attack takes place.

- **Heap Buffer Overflow**

  A tree-oriented data structure, wherein the tree is entirely a binary tree, is known as a heap. After the memory is assigned to the heap while data is written to that memory, having failed to analyze the boundary, a heap buffer overflow attack takes place in the heap data area.

Code Injection Attacks

Through injecting malicious codes within a system, attackers are able to exploit an existing vulnerability: this sort of attack is referred to as a code injection attack. Many of the attacks mentioned in the OWASP Top 10 list happen to be a code injection attack, including the top entry. Such attacks pose one of the greatest threats and require arduous efforts to patch the severe vulnerabilities arising due to it. Code injection attacks can be of three main types.

- **SQL Injections**

  Being one of the most common and critical attacks
  in existence, SQL injection exploits a vulnerability
  in a database. This attack is executed by injecting a
  malicious SQL query into an application or program.
  Even standard SQL queries are manipulated, which
  allows the attacker to exploit unvalidated input
  vulnerabilities within a database. This provides
  unauthorized access to all confidential and critical data
  like passwords, payment details, personal information,
  business documents, and so on. It leads to data theft,
  data manipulation, or data destruction, any of which
  could prove to be harmful to users and organizations.

- **Cross-Site Scripting (XSS)**

  XSS is mostly used to attack a web server by inserting
  malicious PHP or HTML codes into a client-side web
  page or web application, so as to exploit a bug or
  vulnerability. After the victim accesses the compromised
  web page or web app, the malicious script is directed to
  the browser of the victim. XSS attacks are often used for
  data theft and modification of website content.

- **Shell Injection**

  Also known as a *command injection* attack, this takes
  place while you are using a terminal or the shell of
  any system to execute specific commands that require
  input parameters. Attackers intentionally insert
  malicious input that gets executed alongside the code
  or commands you are executing. The malicious inputs
  can be in the form of HTTP headers, cookies, forms,
  etc. Upon executing such arbitrary commands, it can
  cause system compromise or its crashing.

By implementing DevSecOps and defining the security policies within the code itself, most of such vulnerabilities be fixed. Also, by enforcing automation as much as possible, this will prevent manual errors and enable the development and operation team to focus more on the SDLC and ways to merge it with optimum security tools and practices.

Automation with Red Hat Ansible Automation Platform

Organizations can have a hard time going through challenges like delayed-release periods, buggy releases, unsanctioned shadow IT, or unpatched security vulnerabilities. This increases the need for a versatile and resilient platform that will help organizations take back control of their production workflow by automating the infrastructure and deployment workflow. Red Hat Ansible provides organizations with such functionalities by imposing and implementing the standard benchmark approaches while leveraging relevant expertise to be able to provide support to all collaborated teams.

Ansible is undemanding yet an efficiently reliable automation software that can reform the tedious and deficient activities of SDLC in the form of formularized simple and scalable processes. This automation engine can automate application deployment, cloud provisioning, service orchestration, and configuration management so as to allow the development team to allocate their valuable time into the core assigned tasks while also extending support to the operation team to support the process of the DevOps pipeline. Combined, such features can build a fast, thorough, and organized technique to enhance the credibility of an organization.

The primary objective of Ansible is to assure a simplistic and feasible user experience. It highly prioritizes security while staying reliable as it features minimal mobile components, the usability of

OpenSSH, and is based on a language that is easy to learn and use even by non-programmers. Hence this allows users from all domains like development, DevOps, IT management, or system administration, to understand the working of Ansible. It provides users with the capability to manage different environments, from mini-setups with minimum instances up to high-grade heavy environments consisting of several thousand instances.

In Ansible, machines are handled in a way without any agents. As OpenSSH is a well-appraised open source element used throughout the IT industry, the potential security exploits are diminished. Owing to this, upgrading remote daemons or system management issues due to uninstalled daemons are taken care of. The decentralization of Ansible makes it remain reliant on your current OS credentials so as to govern the accessibility of remote systems. Upon requirement, Ansible can be integrated with LDAP, Kerberos (a network authentication protocol), as well as other similar authentication systems.

Figure 3-3 illustrates the architecture of Ansible, presenting its key components and the interconnectivity among them.

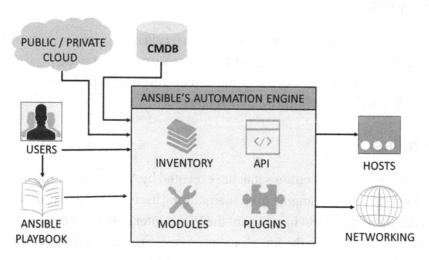

Figure 3-3. *Ansible Architecture*

Ansible Components

So as to understand the working of Ansible and gain a better insight about its usability, it is necessary to get a grasp on some of its crucial concepts.

Control Node

A system with Ansible installed in it is known as a control node. Playbooks and commands can be executed to invoke `/usr/bin/ansible-playbook` or `/usr/bin/ansible` from control nodes, as users can have more than one control node. Systems with preinstalled Python can be used as a control node, making Ansible versatile across multiple devices with the exception of systems running on Windows, which could not be used as a control node.

Managed Nodes

Also referred to as *hosts*, the network devices that are managed with Ansible are known as managed nodes. Managed nodes do not have Ansible installed on them.

Inventory

Inventory is a record of managed nodes. Also called a *hostfile*, inventories can provide, for instance, the IP address of every managed node. Organizing managed nodes, creation, and nesting of groups for better scalability can also be done by an inventory.

Modules

Modules are the code entities that are executed by Ansible. Every module has a specific usage, ranging from maintaining users belonging from a particular database to handling of the VLAN interfaces of a network device. Users will have the functionality of invoking either a single module through a task or various multiple modules within a playbook.

Tasks

Tasks are the elements of action in Ansible. Through an ad hoc command, a particular task can be executed once.

Playbooks

A playbook in Ansible can be defined as a systematic record of tasks that are saved so as to execute them frequently in that specific order. A playbook can also consist of variables along with tasks. Since mostly YAML (or INI) language is used in playbooks, it makes them very simple to read, write, and understand, even by non-programmers.

A usual playbook or a command in Ansible can perform the following actions:

- Selection of machines for execution using the inventory.

- Connecting to such machines or even network devices/ managed nodes, mostly by SSH.

- Copying single or multiple modules to the machines remotely and later executing the tasks on them.

Using Ansible

Ansible has much broader functionality, but users must understand the basic capabilities prior to figuring out the advanced controls and configurations, as well as the processes of orchestrating and deploying.

Ansible extracts the information regarding the machines that you would need to manage. Even though you can provide an IP address via an ad hoc command, it is always better to exploit the convenience of an inventory that is very flexible and provides consistency.

To work with a basic inventory, create or edit the `/etc/ansible/hosts` file and append some remote systems into it by using either an IP address or an FQDN.

```
192.168.0.1
randomserver.xyz.com
randomsystem.xyz.com
```

An inventory can be used to store much more than just FQDNs and IP addresses. You are allowed to use created aliases and even set the variable values for single as well as multiple hosts through *host vars* and *group vars* respectively.

Ansible establishes communication with remote systems via the SSH protocol. Native OpenSSH is used by default to maintain a connection with these remote systems availing the existing username, similar to SSH.

While connecting to all the nodes, you should ensure that you use the same username for the connection. You can also try adding your public SSH key in the `authorized_keys` file, on those nodes, as per the requirements. After the connection is established, modules needed by the playbook or an ad hoc command are migrated to remote systems by Ansible to be executed.

Figure 3-4 represents the general workflow of Ansible. As observed, the management node is in charge of operating the playbook. A list of hosts from the inventory are delivered to the management node to execute the Ansible modules on them. Later, an ssh connection is made by the management node to execute the little modules on the host systems and install the application. After the installation, the modules are retracted by Ansible while a connection is made to the host system to execute the instructions.

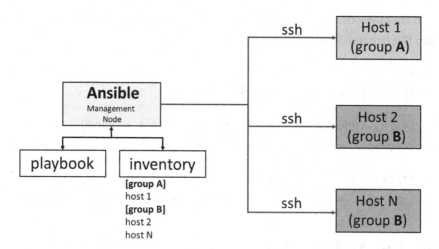

Figure 3-4. *Basic workflow of Ansible*

To ping the nodes in the inventory, use the following command:

```
$ ansible all -m ping
```

To check the implementation, you can run the command:

```
$ ansible all -a "/bin/echo test"
```

An output like below can be viewed for every host in the inventory:

```
randomserver.xyz.com | SUCCESS => {
    "ansible_facts": {
        "discovered_interpreter_python": "/usr/bin/python"
    },
    "changed": false,
    "ping": "pong"
}
```

To execute commands with escalated privileges like as *sudo*, you have to use the *become* flag:

```
# as stark
$ ansible all -m ping -u stark

# as stark, sudoing to root (sudo is default method)
$ ansible all -m ping -u stark --become

# as stark, sudoing to ironman
$ ansible all -m ping -u stark --become --become-user ironman
```

Building an Inventory

Ansible can handle several managed nodes (hosts) simultaneously in an infrastructure by making use of a list or inventory. After an inventory is specified, patterns are utilized to adopt the groups or hosts that are to be managed by Ansible.

The default location of the inventory is /etc/ansible/hosts file. However, this default location can be altered by mentioning another inventory file through the command line applying the -i <path> flag. As a user, you can also be using numerous inventory files in unison while also being able to extract inventory files from the cloud or other environments, or even from other various formats like INI or YAML.

As mentioned, inventory files are created in many formats, based on the chosen plug-ins for inventory. The widely used formats are INI and YAML. The /etc/ansible/hosts file in the INI format can be like the sample provided below.

```
mail.xyz.com

[webservers]
birds.xyz.com
animals.xyz.com
```

```
[dbservers]
uno.xyz.com
dos.xyz.com
tres.xyz.com
```

The same inventory file in YAML format would be like:

```
all:
  hosts:
    mail.xyz.com:
  children:
    webservers:
      hosts:
        birds.xyz.com:
        animals.xyz.com:
    dbservers:
      hosts:
        uno.xyz.com:
        dos.xyz.com:
        tres.xyz.com:
```

Default Groups

Groups can be classified into two default categories: *all* and *ungrouped*. On one hand, as implied from the name, every single host is included in the *all* group. On the other hand, every group that does not belong to any other group except *all* are in the *ungrouped* group. Each host would always be a member of a minimum of two groups, either *all*-or-*ungrouped,* or *all*-or-any different group. Although both of these groups are usually available, their constant and inferred nature prevents them from appearing in group listings like *group_names*.

Like most users, you are bound to include every host in at least two groups. For instance, a development database server in a data center in Texas may also be added in groups named [dev], [texas] and/or [databases]. A group to keep a track of the following can also be made.

- What

  A program, heap, or microservice (Ex. web servers, database servers, etc.).

- Where

  A region or location (data center) to communicate with the local storage, DNS, etc. (Ex. Right, Left).

- When

  The phase of development, to refrain from utilizing the production resources for testing. (Ex. test, prod, sample, etc).

  The earlier mentioned inventory file in YAML can be used as an example to depict the application of *what*, *where*, and *when*.

```
all:
  hosts:
    mail.xyz.com:
  children:
    webservers:
      hosts:
          birds.xyz.com:
          animals.xyz.com:
    dbservers:
      hosts:
          uno.xyz.com:
```

```
        dos.xyz.com:
        tres.xyz.com:
left:
  hosts:
        birds.xyz.com:
        uno.xyz.com:
        dos.xyz.com:
right:
  hosts:
        animals.xyz.com:
        tres.xyz.com:
test:
  hosts:
        birds.xyz.com:
        uno.xyz.com:
        dos.xyz.com:
prod:
  hosts:
        animals.xyz.com:
        tres.xyz.com:
```

Multiple hosts with an identical pattern can be added in the form of a range (numeric or alphabetic) instead of mentioning every host individually. A YAML script for the same would look something like this:

```
...
    webservers:
        hosts:
            www[01:70].xyz.com:
        dbservers:
        hosts:
            db-[c:r].xyz.com
```

Assigning a variable to a particular host can make it efficient to be used later on through the playbooks. In YAML the script can be written as:

```
texas:
  host1:
    http_port: 80
    maxRequestsPerChild: 808
  host2:
    http_port: 303
    maxRequestsPerChild: 909
```

Aliases can also be defined in an inventory:

```
...
  hosts:
    jumper:
      ansible_port: 3333
      ansible_host: 192.168.1.10
```

In the script mentioned above, executing Ansible using the host alias 'jumper' will make the connection to 192.168.1.10 on port 3333. However, for this to work, either the hosts need to have static IP addresses or through a connection that can be secured via tunneling.

In case every host within a group is sharing a variable value, that variable can be applied to the complete group altogether.

```
texas:
  hosts:
    host1:
    host2:
  vars:
    ntp_server: ntp.texas.xyz.com
    proxy: proxy.texas.xyz.com
```

One of the appropriate methods to associate variables to more than one host is through group variables. Prior to its implementation, Ansible usually performs flattening of the variables up to the host level, inclusive of the inventory variables. If any host belongs to more than one group, the variable values from all of its parent groups are read by Ansible. Furthermore, if dissimilar values are assigned to the same variable in various other groups, Ansible selects the aptest value depending upon the internal merging rules.

Ansible Playbook

The YAML format is usually used to depict playbooks, which has minimal syntax. This is to avoid classifying it as a programming language and instead be considered as a configuration operation.

Every playbook comprises single or multiple *plays* within a list. The objective of a play is mapping host groups to specified roles, which are represented by *tasks*. A *task* can be described as a summoning that is made to an Ansible module.

When more than one *play* is used in a playbook, deployments for several machines can be orchestrated by executing specific steps on every machine in the webservers group, next to specific steps on the group of database servers, subsequently again on the webservers group, and so forth. Various plays can be executed at various times.

Figure 3-5 illustrates the structure of an Ansible Playbook and its operation.

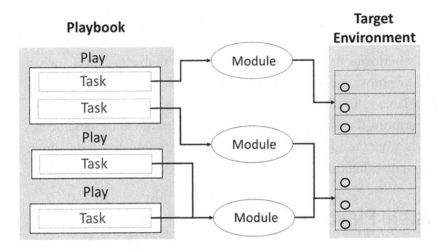

Figure 3-5. *Ansible Playbook*

The following is a playbook example of verify-apache.yml consisting of only one play:

```
...
- hosts: webservers
  vars:
    http_port: 80
    max_clients: 200
  remote_user: root
  tasks:
  - name: ensure apache is at the latest version
    yum:
      name: httpd
      state: latest
  - name: write the apache config file
    template:
      src: /srv/httpd.j2
      dest: /etc/httpd.conf
    notify:
```

```
    - restart apache
- name: ensure apache is running
  service:
    name: httpd
    state: started
  handlers:
    - name: restart apache
      service:
        name: httpd
        state: restarted
```

There can also be more than one play in a playbook, an example for which is provided below:

```
...
- hosts: webservers
  remote_user: root

  tasks:
  - name: ensure apache is at the latest version
    yum:
      name: httpd
      state: latest
  - name: write the apache config file
    template:
      src: /srv/httpd.j2
      dest: /etc/httpd.conf

- hosts: databases
  remote_user: root

  tasks:
  - name: ensure postgresql is at the latest version
    yum:
      name: postgresql
```

```
    state: latest
- name: ensure that postgresql is started
  service:
    name: postgresql
    state: started
```

Using this pattern, users will be able to shift among the targeted host group, user logged into remote servers, considering gaining sudo access, etc. Similar to tasks, even plays are executed in the top to bottom order.

The mentioned examples are just to provide a glimpse of what Ansible is, its functionality, and how the automation properties can be integrated to exploit its features. There are much wider use cases of all the Ansible entities, among which the basics of inventories and playbooks was better described. In order to gain an in-depth understanding of Ansible, you are recommended to refer to its documentation.

DevSecOps in OpenShift

Red Hat OpenShift Container Platform is a container orchestration platform for the development and deployment of containerized applications. It assists the development team with a convenient, reliable, and swift SDLC in various types of environments like public, private, or hybrid. Progressing through the life cycle from the development stage to enterprise-grade production workflow, the emphasis on consistent scanning and overlooking security, increases.

The transient property of containers combined with its scalability poses a challenge to record the functioning strength of the services deriving from each container. Along with analyzing every container separately, it's equally crucial to monitor these containers together as part of clusters. This will provide a deeper insight into their interactivity with one another, especially considering how microservices extend across several containers and applications.

Continuous Security must be an important factor in the DevSecOps, like CI and CD. Ensuring compliance of all the security protocols throughout the life cycle is a necessity. The practice of continuous security in container orchestration platforms focuses on three main aspects.

- **Provenance**

  To determine the inception of an application and container attributes like source code, build, or test reports.

- **Visibility**

  To monitor the functional performance of services and ensure the safety of the infrastructure.

- **Forensics**

  To analyze and troubleshoot the root causes of service availability, potentially abruptive outgoing connections, and data amended on disk.

At least a few features need to be implemented while using Red Hat OpenShift Container Platform so as to integrate intrinsic security measures within the critical stages of the workflow.

- Static and dynamic analysis, and vulnerability assessments of the image and external repositories.

- Ensuring compliance and cross-verification of the security standards like NVD, NIST, CVE, ISO, OWASP, PCI DSS, and similar.

- Telemetry surveillance and alert systems.

- Zero-day vulnerability avoidance and detection.

- Logging and frequent auditing.

Red Hat Consulting

Organizations are always recommended to plan, design, and build their infrastructure themselves, to help retain the flexibility and expertise regarding the architecture. However, in dire scenarios, organizations can also prefer opting for Red Hat Consulting that will assist them build the optimum infrastructure as per their requirements.

Red Hat uses a strategy known as the Solution Delivery Framework (SDF), which helps users with better ROI during an infrastructure creation.

Red Hat Consulting facilitates the building of improved infrastructure, by merging open source programs and specifications, commercial insights, enterprise expertise, and validated techniques. It will help organizations with modernizing virtualized infrastructures, migration to an adaptable and scalable cloud environment, utilizing an efficient storage solution, or even enhancing the agility of an organization through container deployments on the cloud.

Through this, the service delivery of containerized applications can be hastened and automated while improving the coherence through the implementation of a standardized operating environment.

## CHAPTER 4

Red Hat Hyperconverged Infrastructure

This chapter aims to highlight hyperconverged infrastructure, its concepts, operations, and how to ensure its security.

Obsolescence of Legacy Infrastructure

The IT landscape of data center infrastructures are ever changing, which encourages the development of newer, better, and more efficient solutions. Such solutions are required to be sufficient for the growing business needs, which make them more suitable than current technology. Hyperconvergence is one such solution that can be defined as the building of private data center that strive for the emulation of public cloud consumption, with respect to lucid functionality, granular scalability, and economic modeling. Enhanced features like these are provided without compromising other essential factors available in the existing methods.

The legacy infrastructure that primarily consists of network, storage, and servers is often referred to as the three-tiered infrastructure. This three-tiered model has been in use for a long period of time but is no

© Rithik Chatterjee 2021
R. Chatterjee, *Red Hat and IT Security*,
https://doi.org/10.1007/978-1-4842-6434-8_4

longer able to cope with the growing technological needs. Many experts are now considering this infrastructure to have become archaic, thus requiring a modern solution like Hyperconvergence.

What Is Hyperconverged Infrastructure?

Hyperconverged Infrastructure (HCI) is a coalesced system that amalgamates every component of a conventional data center like computing, networking, storage, and management with smart applications. The integration among these components builds building blocks with the required flexibility for replacing the legacy systems, comprising detached storage arrays, networks, and servers.

A basic HCI can be described as an assortment of storage, servers, and virtualization. HCI workloads run within the VM; however, recent versions of HCI have enabled support for native containerization too.

The data center stack that includes computing, storage, networking, and virtualization in its entirety is converged by HCI. Legacy infrastructures, which can also be comparatively more complex, are being reformed with an improved platform that is run by the turnkey, enterprise-grade servers that allow organizations to begin slowly and gradually scale each node as per the requirements. Entire operating functions are transmitted over the cluster by applications executed on every server node, to enhance the potential and increase the flexibility. Figure 4-1 illustrates the basic structure of the traditional infrastructure against the evolved architecture of a hyperconverged infrastructure.

Traditional Infrastructure   Hyperconverged Infrastructure

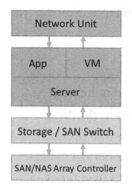
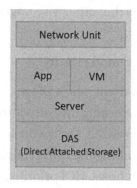

Figure 4-1. *Traditional Infrastructure vs. Hyperconverged Infrastructure*

There are two primary elements of HCI: the Management Plane and the Distributed Plane.

- The management plane is responsible for regulating the HCI resources through a centralized manner, which thus extinguishes the requirement for individual solutions to manage SANs, storages, networks, virtualization, and servers.

- The distributed plane is executed over a node cluster providing virtualization, networking, and storage for the external solutions, be it a VM or a containerized application. The distributed plane performs the abstraction of the computing, storage, and networking resources.

Usually, all HCI solutions are entirely software defined without any reliability on exclusive hardware. Every individual HCI node within a cluster executes a VM while the control features of HCI are run as an autonomous VM on all nodes, which can act as a single entity performing scalability of resources, adding new nodes.

107

Adapting to a hyperconverged infrastructure will provide users with many benefits that otherwise might not be available from the traditional infrastructure.

- Workload Priority

  For many years, the management and policies concerning infrastructures have been improperly prioritized. Unlike the legacy systems that prefer handling the LUNs (Logical Unit Numbers), clusters, and hosts, HCI prioritizes applications over other factors.

- Efficient Data Management

  HCI functionality enables a high rate of data reduction through methods like compression and deduplication. This results in better accessible needs for the bandwidth of network, IOPS requirements, and storage capacity.

- Resilience

  One of the best features of cloud computing is scalability, whether vertically or horizontally as per the requirements. HCI takes advantage of this cloud feature and emphasizes more on this to ensure ease of scalability, in miniscule units.

- Data Security

  The core concept of hyperconvergence is to streamline and merge infrastructure resources. Hence, instead of managing an unattached backup and recovery system, HCI usually has this crucial technique as a built-in feature. This provides centralized and improved data security, even for the backups.

- Faster Drives

    HCI offers better and enhanced performance with the
    usage of SSD disks.

- Efficient Deployments

    Hyperconvergence facilitates quicker and effortless
    deployments.

- Automated Redundancy

    HCI enables the data center for an automated
    allocation of infrastructure resources in the event of
    any hardware failures.

The hyperconvergence technology is not actually a brand new strategy
as it is a successor of the convergence model. The model was essentially
developed to overcome the challenges associated with tangled complexity
and excess interrelationships. However, it was soon deemed necessary to
seek an evolved version due to many of its limitations like hardware dealer
lock-ins, arduous upgrading because of interconnectivity dependencies,
complex scalability, and higher costs.

HCI or Hyperconvergence has had a higher effect on the hypervisor
(VM model) market. What was once an exclusive enterprise solution has
now been equalized and commercialized, since numerous HCI vendors are
now developing their own hypervisors, initiating from the open source KVM.

HCI Architecture

As the primary focus during the development of hyperconvergence was
storage, it is manageable in either of two ways, with or without a controller
VM. Naturally, each option has its own merits and demerits. Considering
the first approach, using a controller VM provides increased flexibility. The
hypervisor does not need much attention from the controller VM because
of its independent functionality to handle the host storage operations.

One of the major demerits of such models is their overconsumption of resources and adding an auxiliary component in the data path, which is often absent from other architectures. Even so, its influence has been reduced a lot mostly because of more powerful CPUs. The approach of controller VM is resource heavy as it utilizes RAM and CPU cores up to its maximum extent; despite that, the merits derived from it more than compensate for such costs. The VM controls the data deduplication activities, which demand RAM and CPU cycles in order to store excess metadata. This, in turn, provides data reduction, which when considered, higher RAM usage can be compromised in exchange for a lowered amount of overall data volume.

Also, because of evolving technology, the financial overhead for this architecture has decreased. Current technology involves a CPU with many cores, hence trading off a few of them to manage data storage operations more efficiently and reduce hardware complexity is the optimum solution.

The other method of storage management in HCI enables a hypervisor kernel module or even just a kernel module to control the storage operations. Although this improves the overall functionality, you will be restrained to a single hypervisor usage. Users often wind up enforced, to use an overpriced application in the ecosystem, despite it not being the preferable option.

To top it off, a few of the applications demand high RAM utilization for the metadata tables associated with data reduction. Thus, this may lead to sparing some CPU cores from any overheads, but it will not have any substantial effect on the RAM requirement.

Eventually, both approaches are bound to have identical conclusions. HCI cluster provisions storage, which can practically replace the dedicated resources that called for an assigned team and skills for management. Features like data reduction and encryption do not cause hardware overheads, as the features have developed to transform into software-oriented ones, which can exploit the maximum capability of the existing low-cost hardware while gaining the exact results, if not better.

Users have the freedom to choose between opting for hardware with preinstalled hyperconvergence or go for a hardware environment that will be compatible and support the development of HCI. Post that, HCI clusters can be built that provisions a failsafe and accessibility system, useful during any possible malfunction.

Gradually, additional nodes can be introduced and connected to the cluster. The underlying management function is responsible for managing the gritty task of data availability, that too, to the relevant VMs. Through the blend of existing hardware functions and software proficiency, redundancy can be achieved, which ensures that data is available on a minimum of two nodes within the cluster, at any given time.

There are multiple use cases of HCI that have benefited organizations, a few of which are listed below.

Databases

A database is the core element of any infrastructure that is used to store all the critical data in an organized tabular format. There are wide uses of it, but one of the common factors of databases is its ability to provide high performance, especially for platforms like e-commerce or payment gateways. As it is the bottom-most element, its performance is directly proportional to the efficiency of the infrastructure, thereby affecting an organization financially. Hyperconverged Infrastructure is adept in managing even the most critical of database platforms because of its usage of flash storage and the competence of storage per node in the cluster. Besides that, HCI also enables organizations to scale up their storage units with ease by connecting additional nodes. This feature of customizable scalability is one of the advantages that HCI has over the traditional infrastructures.

Analytics and Logging

Over time, analytics and logging are one of the main aspects that have had an increased impact upon the IT team of any organization. Tools pertaining to these functions have distinct features. The core infrastructure must be capable enough to handle a substantial proportion of data velocity, like high data read-writes. Along with that, it is also critical to be able to facilitate swift storage scalability since logging can require enormous storage space.

Analytics has analogous attributes such as the sort of data or workload created based on the utilization. To analyze it, collecting data is important, after which data mining is required for discerning the relevance of data. HCI is more equipped to support such comprehensive tasks with proper configurations. By deploying an apt hyperconverged architecture along with all-flash or hybrid nodes, a higher grade of performance can be achieved.

Data Security

Data security is not just about ensuring the availability of data but also being able to secure it, especially from unauthorized accesses. This also includes the provision of extensive disaster recovery strategies to secure data while maintaining its redundancy. HCI platforms have expertise in data security. With high scalability, providing high-grade security services for data should not be an issue. Lately, the use of secondary storage is becoming the norm to enable features like redundancy and backup recovery. HCI environments offer secondary storage through scalable storage and centralized workload management.

Data Storage

Many organizations have file servers to store any excess data but most importantly also to store the confidential business-related documents and files. It is up to the IT team to warrant the availability and security of such resources. As file servers are required mostly to store data, performance is not really a criterion for it. Contrarily, the storage volume is a critical aspect for file servers. Data ranging from mini-reports to business videos or frameworks and libraries may be stored in these file servers. To scale up the storage volume in HCI, you will need to connect additional nodes. Even native file services can be included in an HCI platform, which provides simplicity and high scalability. By integrating the services and resources to a domain controller, the platform can enable a centralized and secure authentication system.

Edge Computing

Edge computing is a computational model that involves conducting computations near the data source itself, so as to conserve bandwidth and refine the response time. Here, the term 'edge' translates as geographic distribution. From an organizational standpoint, edge computing can be described as the computing tasks that are conducted outside of their own data centers or cloud infrastructures. The locations may be remote sites or different office branches; however, it may also include spots like automated self-driven vehicles, or similar IoT devices. Since HCI can be initiated with small setups, its implementation in remote sites or branch locations would be efficient. Simplicity and convenient scalability are an advantage for such use cases. Several edge infrastructures do not have any assigned IT team; hence a deployed HCI will provide robust and reliable administration with the option of being easily scalable. With a standard basic HCI architecture, it will also be a cost-effective solution for organizations, especially considering its key features.

113

Desktop as a Service (DaaS)

DaaS and VDI (Virtual Desktop Infrastructure) eases administrators with desktop virtualization. It is what admins use to manage remote servers and environments. Despite its features, there are key limitations, like malfunctioning VDIs caused by subpar storage coupled with complicated architecture. With the implementation of HCI, all the components of VDI have all been amassed into a single platform. It also provides ample storage to help organizations with issues concerning booting and logging into the systems, which was usually a challenge in the previous technology. This made VDI a very prime application of HCI platforms.

DaaS is a form of SaaS (Software as a Service), and early versions of it allowed users to use their desktops through the cloud. On-prem DaaS using HCI can ensure additional flexibility while enabling organizations to preserve an on-prem desktop environment along with the existing features of DaaS.

Programming

It is highly essential for the development and testing team to utilize enterprise-grade software and tools considering the criticality of their role. The hyperconvergence platform provides the development team with a computational infrastructure environment that can be incorporated in the SDLC. With virtualization flexibility, VMs can be built and terminated, on suitable environments, all as per the organizational requirements.

General Uses

Apart from specific use cases, HCI also has been valuable in prevalent regular enterprise needs. Almost all organizations have such standard requirements as DHCP, domain controller, DNS, and other types of servers too. General usage can include every possible operational and infrastructural need of an organization. As vague as this may seem, the hyperconvergence technology genuinely has real-time applications for a wide array of use cases, which is why many companies are now adopting it.

Red Hat Hyperconverged Infrastructure for Virtualization

Simplified integration of computation, storage, and networking infrastructure has made HCI a desirable option for many organizations. For virtualized platforms, Red Hat Hyperconverged Infrastructure proves to be a viable solution. Red Hat HCI provides a simplified method for designing and acquisition while modernizing the product releases and management. It enables efficiency by ensuring a one-time life cycle as an ordeal part of the virtualized computation and storage elements. Organizations have the flexibility to choose from open source resources and enterprise-grade hardware while applying verified configurations based on specific requirements.

Red Hat HCI enables evolved data reduction techniques, vGPU, and application-specified network features. Red Hat HCI for Virtualization enables the following:

- Provision of uncomplicated virtualization for enterprise applications, increasing the usage of resources up to the full extent via the merging of infrastructure components, achieving proficient functionality.

- Deployment of efficient and flexible application-defined infrastructure.

- Management of cohesive computational and storage entities through the same user interface.

- Installation of a general operating environment for third-party service vendors.

With evolving technology, computational and storage resources are always in demand, especially for the development, operations, and administration teams. In domains like banking, finance, retail, or handling remote sites, they often require functionality akin to what hyperconvergence offers - mostly because such domains do not necessarily have a dedicated IT team to manage the technical operations. Hence, they require an environment with a minimal physical footprint and uncomplicated operational and management administration.

Red Hat HCI for Virtualization comprises enterprise-validated resources of the Red Hat stack. The resources are exclusively configured and integrated for deploying on the exact servers, which minimizes the physical footprint, thus preserving time required for deployment while ensuring a simplified and seamless functionality. Red Hat has always been about promoting open source technologies to the consumers, and Red Hat HCIv provides immense flexibility, specifically in deployable configurations, with its core solutions as a foundation:

- **Red Hat Virtualization**

  Developed on RHEL and KVM (Kernel-based Virtual Machine), Red Hat Virtualization provides virtualization for both Linux and Microsoft Windows. It is able to virtualize processes, resources, and applications, which results in stability for containerized and cloud-native applications.

- **Red Hat Storage**

  Similar to Red Hat Virtualization, Red Hat Storage is a software-defined platform designed specifically for storage of high-end activities similar to virtualization. Contrary to legacy storage environments, Red Hat Storage can be scaled over basic hardware, virtualized, and containerized deployments.

- **Red Hat Ansible Automation Platform**

  To reiterate, Ansible is a standard agentless automation platform through which users can perform streamlined deployments while having centralized management for remote clusters.

Integrated with these core solutions, Red Hat HCI for Virtualization has much more benefits than just untangling the legacy infrastructure that includes resources like storage, computation, and networking.

- Default inbuilt predictability from testing and functioning, specified through use cases,

- Cost-effectiveness due to unification and normalization of infrastructure resources,

- Low preliminary expenditure for PoCs (Proof of Concepts),

- Simple installation, maintenance, and management of the solution,

- Enterprise-grade scalability options and flexibility.

Core Operations

Red Hat HCI for Virtualization provides resilient features of data reduction derived from compression and deduplication. This enables vGPU support and compatibility with software-defined networking.

- Data Reduction

  Many enterprises have numerous VMs based on their vast demands, often decreasing the redundancy of stored data. Red Hat HCIv is able to decrease the expenditure related to aggregation of huge volumes of

117

data. In the technique, there exists VDO (Virtual Data Optimizer) module with the Linux device mapper, as provisioned in RHEL. The VDO module is responsible for delivering real-time, controlled, block-level compression and deduplication at 4KB level along with managing the VDO data reduction.

- Open Virtual Network (OVN)

  One of the key elements of HCI is software-defined networking. To segregate the logical network from the tangible network topology, OVN is utilized, which is an open source virtual switching model. It enhances the scalability while expediting real-time migration of virtual network elements, in the absence of any VM interference.

- vGPU compatibility

  Companies in domains like oil and gas require efficient methods to provide intricate graphics accompanied by high-grade refined performance virtualized systems. Ensuring vGPU compatibility enables enterprises to elevate the visual precision, upgrade the performance, and lower the latency while providing virtual graphics to remote users.

Red Hat HCI for Virtualization enhances the functioning proficiency via fusing and integrating the primary servers. Two virtualization hosts and storage hosts can be merged along with the management environment to create two physical servers with the same management interface.

Key Features

Below are the key features:

- Centralized Management of Virtual Resources

- Security via Encryption

- High Resource Availability

- Automated Operations

- Guest OS Compatibility

Red Hat Virtualization

A software-defined and open platform, Red Hat Virtualization is primarily used to virtualize Linux and Windows environments. With RHEL and KVM as its foundation, Red Hat Virtualization equips tools for managing the virtual resources, applications, services, and processes, which acts as a robust base for containerized and cloud-native applications.

Users can deploy Red Hat Virtualization in the form of a self-hosted engine or even as a stand-alone manager. Usually it is advisable to opt for the self-hosted engine as a preferred mode of deployment.

In case of a self-hosted engine environment, the Red Hat Virtualization Manager is executed as a VM on engine nodes that are self-hosted and are referred to as specialized nodes, within the singular environment it is responsible for managing. This form of environment reduces the need for a supplemental physical server but, in turn, demands additional administrative overhead for deployment and management. The manager provides high availability despite any absence of an extrinsic HA management. Figure 4-2 illustrates the architecture of this self-hosted engine in Red Hat Virtualization.

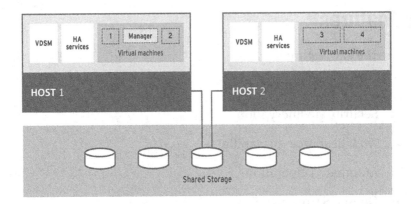

Figure 4-2. *Red Hat Virtualization Self-Hosted Engine Architecture*

In a stand-alone manager setup, the Red Hat Virtualization Manager is run either on a physical server or on a VM that is hosted in a different virtualized environment. Unlike a self-hosted engine, a stand-alone manager is comparatively simple in terms of deploying and managing but also calls for the usage of an extra physical server. A solution like *High Availability Add-On* by Red Hat is required to ensure constant availability of the manager. Figure 4-3 illustrates the architecture of this stand-alone manager in Red Hat Virtualization.

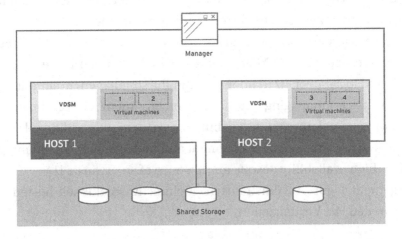

Figure 4-3. *Red Hat Virtualization Stand-Alone Manager Architecture*

Elements of Red Hat Virtualization

This section covers the important elements of Red Hat Virtualization.

Cluster

A group of physical hosts acting as a pool of resources for VMs is known as a cluster. The same storage and networking are utilized by all the hosts within a cluster. These result in the creation of a migration domain and the hosts inside it can be shifted from one host to another.

Data center

The top-level container for every physical and logical resource residing in a controlled virtualized environment is known as a data center. This is a stack of VMs, clusters, networks, and storage domains.

Event

An event can be classified as an alert, warning, or other notification about various activities that aid the admins in controlling the monitoring, functionality, and status of the components.

HA Services

The `ovirt-ha-agent` service and the `ovirt-ha-broker` service are encompassed in the HA services. It is executed on self-hosted engine nodes and controls the increased availability of the manager VM.

Host

A host, also referred to as a hypervisor, can be defined as a physical server on which a single or several VMs are executed and these hosts are stacked into clusters. Inside a cluster, there could be a migration of VMs from a host to another. Full virtualization can be achieved by making use of a loaded Linux kernel module known as a Kernel-based Virtual Machine (KVM). VMs are run on the host system and controlled remotely by the RHV Manager.

Storage Pool Manager (SPM)

SPM is a profile allotted to a particular host within a data center. All the metadata modifications of the data center, like creating or removing a virtual disk, can only be performed by an SPM.

Host Storage Manager (HSM)

HSM is a host in a data center that is not a Storage Pool Manager (SPM) and can be utilized for operating data, like shifting a disk among storage domains. This would help avoid any constriction at the SPM host, which is meant to be used for brief metadata tasks.

Networking

All functions like user connections, host management, VM connectivity, and storage, are dependent on a network infrastructure that is properly designed, executed, and configured to provide high-grade performance. RHV differentiates network traffic by establishing logical networks. The logical model of a physical network is known as a logical network. It includes the connections and network traffic among the manager, hosts, VMs, and storage. These logical networks determine the supposedly suitable route to be followed by the selected type of network traffic. The purpose of their creation is to separate the network traffic based on performance or even for physical topology virtualization.

Self-Hosted Engine Node

A host with an installed self-hosted engine packaged to host the Manager VM is a Self-hosted Engine Node. Usual nodes can be connected to self-hosted engine environments as well; however, they would not be able to host the Manager VM.

Template

A model VM with preset configurations is called a template. A VM that is built using a template will inherit the configurations that are set for that template. Templates are used for mass creation of multiple VMs in just one step.

Data Warehouse

The data warehouse in Red Hat Virtualization gathers the data being monitored on VMs, hosts, and storage. It includes a database along with a service, and it needs installation and configuration like the setup of the Manager, which can be done on the same system or a different server.

For proper calculation and estimation of the resources and storage, the Data Warehouse (`ovirt_engine_history`) database will utilize the following tool: Red Hat Virtualization History Database Size Calculator. It calculates the number of components and time duration decided by the user to maintain the history records and assist with determining the estimation.

Metrics Store

The metrics store gathers all metrics and logs generated in RHV. The data is later moved from RHV to OpenShift, while the data is accumulated in Elasticsearch and retained in the indexes in OpenShift. Post that, Kibana is used to visualize and analyze the data.

Elasticsearch is an open source RESTful and distributed analytics engine that addresses a wide variety of use cases, allowing users to merge and carry out multiple search types.

Kibana is an open source platform for data visualization and analytics, developed to be worked while integrated with Elasticsearch. Users will be able to execute acute data analysis and visualize it in the form of charts and tables.

Security in Red Hat Virtualization

Red Hat Virtualization enables organizations to alleviate the associated threats through multiple techniques as mentioned below.

- Control Groups

  Red Hat Virtualization consists of a kernel feature and other tools that are in charge of allocating and isolating the resources. Using this feature, resource limiting can be made use of, along with accounting measurements and operating via prioritizing.

- SELinux

  SELinux is a key component of Red Hat Virtualization as it is derived from RHEL itself. SELinux is a Linux security module and using it, mandatory access control can be enforced across the system. All processes and files are labeled as per the enforcement, apart from which SELinux also enables restrictions suitable for each role and type.

- Encryption

  Red Hat Virtualization uses SSL and TLS for encryption throughout its environment. All traffic is thus encrypted, reducing any potential attack surface.

The key parts of security in Red Hat Virtualization are SELinux and sVirt. SELinux enables the admins to enforce custom security policies on executable processes and its operations.

sVirt ensures that the labeling scheme of SELinux is also applicable to VMs, utilizing its security abilities to secure the environment. The processes of the VM are dynamically labeled as per the implemented policies on the file images, restricting the processes for accessing external resources themselves. The policy labels are automated and are dynamically executed to remove dependency on manual administration while enforcing a systemwide policy-oriented security strategy.

libvirt, which is a virtualization management abstraction layer, is integrated with sVirt for provisioning a MAC framework for VMs. Through this architecture, interfunctionality can be implemented between every libvirt compatible virtualization platform and every sVirt compatible MAC implementation.

Configuration of sVirt

For configuration of sVirt, SELinux Booleans are used. They are toggle variables that can be switched off or on, allowing it to enable/disable further conditions.

While toggling the Booleans, for changing temporarily, use:

```
# setsebool boolean_name {on|off}
```

and for changing permanently (across reboots), use:

```
# setsebool -P boolean_name {on|off}
```

To display the running state of the Booleans, use:

```
# getsebool -a|grep virt
```

To display all the SELinux Booleans, use:

```
# getsebool -a | less
```

Similar to other services operated with SELinux, sVirt leverages restrictions, labels, and process-oriented methods that deliver enhanced security and guest access control. Resources are applied labels by default depending on the latest functioning VM (this method is termed as dynamic), and it can be applied manually too: by enabling admins to specify it as per their requirements (this method is termed as static).

Flexibility with Red Hat Gluster Storage

Red Hat Gluster Storage (previously known as Red Hat Storage Server) is a software-defined, open and scalable platform, developed to control unorganized data and be deployable on virtual, physical, and cloud and even containerized environments. This SDS (software-defined storage) platform is designed to manage routine usage workloads such as backup, recovery, analytics, and archiving too. This makes Gluster Storage optimum for hyperconverged infrastructure. Being a cost-effective solution, Red Hat Gluster Storage is a combination of object and file storage, with a scalable architecture that has the capacity to handle data in a scale of petabytes.

Various types of unorganized data are stored using Red Hat Gluster Storage, such as the following:

- Heavy media files, namely, images, audio, and video files.

- Backup image files and archiving.

- Logs of big data, RFID data, and similar system-produced data.

- VM images.

With RHEL as its foundation, Red Hat Gluster Storage allows users to adopt a cost-efficient solution without any trade-offs in the scalability of the operational functionality and is also compatible with widely used x86 servers. Storage silos are diminished by enabling universal access to the data via several objects and file protocols.

With the constant evolution of containerization and cloud-native environments, the demand for similar features akin to virtualized environments will keep rising. Stateful applications will also need its application data to gain a high-availability exterior to its native containers.

There are two general alternatives to facilitate persistent data storage for containerized applications enabled by Red Hat Gluster Storage.

- Connecting distributed SDS in the form of a network-connected storage cluster to the RHOCP cluster. This will enable applications to have data persistence in a premium-level storage repository, which is POSIX (Portable Operating System Interface) compatible.

- Another alternative is to have a hyperconverged storage within exclusively allocated storage containers, which enables the development team to minutely handle and control the storage by making use of RHOCP as a singular control dashboard. Apart from cost-effectiveness from HCI, this strategy also helps administrators avoid any concerns about storage that is exterior to containers.

One of the primary foundations of the Gluster Storage is GlusterFS, which is derived from a nestable user-space design while being able to provide a remarkable outcome, for varied workload executions. Different storage servers across the network are accumulated and interconnected into a single huge parallel NFS (Network File System). Since the GlusterFS servers are compatible with POSIX, the servers utilize the XFS file system for data storage and they are accessible by protocols like CIFS and NFS.

Red Hat Gluster Storage provides network encryption for better security in networking. The process of network encryption includes conversion of data into an encoded format to ensure a secure data transmission over the network. Through this, unauthorized data access can be prevented.

Gluster Storage makes use of SSL/TLS for network encryption within its authentication and authorization mechanisms, instead of the traditional unencrypted methods. The network encryption includes the following categories:

- **I/O Encryption**

  The I/O connections among the servers and clients of Red Hat Gluster Storage is encrypted.

- **Management Encryption**

  Encryption is performed on the management connections (glusterd) located in a trusted storage pool, and among glusterd and SMB clients or NFS Ganesha.

The configuration of network encryption is carried out through the following files:

- /etc/ssl/glusterfs.pem

- /etc/ssl/glusterfs.key

- /etc/ssl/glusterfs.ca

- /var/lib/glusterd/secure-access

It is usually recommended to enable both I/O and management encryption for better optimized security. To enable the management encryption on a Red Hat Gluster Storage that has been newly deployed without a configured trusted storage pool, the following actions need to be performed on all servers.

A secure access file needs to be created, which can also be empty if default settings are used.

```
# touch /var/lib/glusterd/secure-access
```

Some changes might be required in the settings of the SSL certificate depth as per the specifications of the CA (Certificate Authority). Use the following command and add the CA at the mentioned part.

```
# echo "option transport.socket.ssl-cert-depth EnterYourCAhere"
> /var/lib/glusterd/secure-access
```

Use the following command to start the servers:

```
# systemctl start glusterd
```

Later on, you can perform the regular configuration procedure of formatting and creating storage volumes. This is a prerequisite for enabling management encryption on the client systems.

The following actions need to be performed on all the client systems.

Use this command to create the secure access file:

```
# touch /var/lib/glusterd/secure-access
```

Use the following command to edit the settings of SSL certificate depth:

```
# echo "option transport.socket.ssl-cert-depth EnterYourCAhere"
> /var/lib/glusterd/secure-access
```

To start the volume, use the command:

```
# gluster volume start NameOfVol
```

After starting the volume, it needs to be mounted and that process depends on the native-client protocol. Using the following command, the volume can be mounted using the FUSE protocol:

```
# mount -t glusterfs server1:/NameOfVol /mnt/glusterfs
```

The following actions need to be performed to enable the I/O encryption among the server and the clients. The volumes should be configured but not be in the start mode; if it is started, the following command can be used to stop the volume:

```
# gluster volume stop NameOfVol
```

After stopping the volume, the following commands can be executed from any Gluster server.

A list of common server and client names that are authorized to access the volume has to be provided. The names should be the same as the ones mentioned during the generation of the glusterfs.pem file.

```
# gluster volume set NameOfVol auth.ssl-allow 'server1,server2,
client1,client2,client3'
```

The following commands are to be used for enabling the SSL/TLS on the volume:

```
# gluster volume set NameOfVol client.ssl on
# gluster volume set NameOfVol server.ssl on
```

Use the following command to start the volume:

```
# gluster volume start NameOfVol
```

After the volume is started, the volume mounting on authorized clients should be verified. Similar to management encryption, the mounting process depends on the native-client protocol. Using the following command, the volume can be mounted using the FUSE protocol:

```
# mount -t glusterfs server1:/NameOfVol /mnt/glusterfs
```

For configuration of management and I/O encryption with a deployed Trusted Storage Pool in Red Hat Gluster Storage:

The following steps need to be performed for enabling the I/O encryption.

To proceed, the mounted volume from all the clients have to be unmounted.

```
# umount MountLocation
```

Execute the below command from any server to stop the volume:

```
# gluster volume stop NameOfVol
```

Just like in the previous section, a list of common server and client names that are authorized to access the volume has to be provided.

```
# gluster volume set NameOfVol auth.ssl-allow 'server1,server2,
client1,client2,client3'
```

Use the following commands to enable TLS/SSL encryption:

```
# gluster volume set NameOfVol client.ssl on
# gluster volume set NameOfVol server.ssl on
```

Use the following command to start the volume:

```
# gluster volume start NameOfVol
```

Lastly, use the following command to mount the volume through the native FUSE protocol.

```
# mount -t glusterfs server1:/NameOfVol /mnt/glusterfs
```

For enabling the management encryption with a deployed Trusted Storage Pool, the storage server should be offline. This will require a downtime for all volumes, applications, clients, and also features like geo-replication, and snapshots, which are connected to the storage server.

The following command has to be executed on all clients for every volume that is mounted on those clients.

```
# umount MountLocation
```

Use the command below to stop the NFS-Ganesha/SMB services:

```
# systemctl stop nfs-ganesha
# systemctl stop ctdb
```

Use the following command to unmount any shared storage:

```
# umount /var/run/gluster/shared_storage
```

Use the following command to stop all the volumes:

```
# for vol in 'gluster volume list'; do gluster --mode=script
volume stop $vol; sleep 2s; done
```

Gluster services on all the servers will have to be stopped:

```
# systemctl stop glusterd
# pkill glusterfs
```

After performing the above actions, the following actions will be similar to that of the previous section (management encryption without a configured trusted storage pool); hence only the commands are being mentioned for reference.

```
# touch /var/lib/glusterd/secure-access
# echo "option transport.socket.ssl-cert-depth EnterYourCAhere" >
/var/lib/glusterd/secure-access
# systemctl start glusterd
```

Later, all the volumes have to be started.

```
# for vol in 'gluster volume list'; do gluster --mode=script
volume start $vol; sleep 2s; done
```

Mount any shared storage:

```
# mount -t glusterfs hostname:/gluster_shared_storage /run/
gluster/shared_storage
```

Use the commands below to restart the NFS-Ganesha/SMB services:

```
# systemctl start nfs-ganesha
# systemctl start ctdb
```

Lastly, use the following commands to mount the volumes on clients through the native FUSE protocol:

```
# mount -t glusterfs server1:/NameOfVol /mnt/glusterfs
```

These mentioned steps are to guide you about the process for management and I/O encryption in Red Hat Gluster Storage. For all other procedures associated with the deployment and configurations, you can refer to the documentation of Gluster Storage.

Gluster Storage is deployable in private clouds or data centers through On-Premise Red Hat Gluster Storage Servers. Users would also be able to install it on storage hardware and commodity servers, within a robust, vastly available, and hugely scalable NAS environment. In order for Gluster Storage to be deployed in the public cloud through Red Hat Gluster Storage for Public Cloud, like inside AWS environment, *glusterFS* is packaged as an AMI (Amazon Machine Image), which facilitates the deployment of scalable NAS, in AWS. It is able to provide enterprise-grade operations and attributes desired from a solution in a data center or private cloud to the public cloud by provisioning NAS with high scalability and availability in the cloud.

Figure 4-4 depicts the primary architecture of a single cluster in Red Hat Gluster Storage.

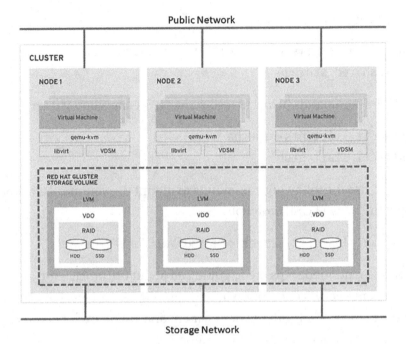

Figure 4-4. *Single Cluster Architecture in Red Hat Gluster Storage*

Here are the key features:

- Increased Scalability

- File Fragmentation

- Cloud and Container Support

- Virtualization

- Exclusive Global Namespace

- Synchronous and Asynchronous Data Replication

- Bit-rot Detection

- Erasure Coding

- Hadoop Integration

Red Hat Hyperconverged Infrastructure for Cloud

Red Hat HCI for Cloud is a blend of Red Hat Ceph Storage and Red Hat OpenStack Platform, creating a merged solution that offers common support and life cycles. Together the operations of storage and computation are executed on the very host as the other, which enables high efficiency and substantial coherence.

The solution of HCI for cloud provides a platform for enhancing application migration among data centers and the edge. Moreover, OpenStack deployment nodes are congruous, enabling users to have the freedom to opt for non-hyperconverged nodes over the networks, having hyperconverged nodes at the edge, thus refining resource usage.

The Red Hat HCI for Cloud consolidates Red Hat Ceph Storage and Red Hat OpenStack Platform, into a single solution in order to achieve three primary objectives:

- Deployment simplification of RHCS and RHOSP.

- Provisioning of higher anticipated performance experience.

- Gain a decreased entrance cost for RHOSP and RHCS, by colocating their individual services on the exact node.

The Red Hat HCI colocating situations can be described as follows:

- The RHCS Monitor services and RHOSP Controller on the same node.

- The RHCS Object Storage Daemon (OSD) services and the RHOSP Nova Compute on the same node.

Figure 4-5 illustrates the cloud architecture in Red Hat Hyperconverged Infrastructure, describing the connection of Red Hat OpenStack Platform Director with controllers and computing/storage nodes.

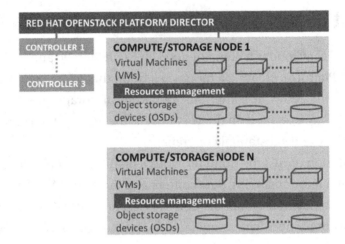

Figure 4-5. *Red Hat Hyperconverged Infrastructure for Cloud Architecture*

Users can choose the deployment of Red Hat HCI for Cloud, either through Red Hat OpenStack Platform Director web GUI or by CLI (command-line interface).

Red Hat HCI for Cloud has the following mentioned distinct features and advantages:

- Decreased Deployment Footprint

- Eliminated Failure Points

- Sole Orchestration Manager

- High Resource Management through KVM (Kernel-based VM) and NUMA (Non-Uniform Memory Access)

- Containerization-oriented Deployment Strategy

- Superior Scalability

- OpenStack and Private Cloud Compatibility

Cloud Computing with Red Hat OpenStack Platform (RHOSP)

Red Hat OpenStack is a platform that is open source and leverages combined virtual resources that are utilized to develop and maintain public and private clouds. There are tools known as *projects* that include the OpenStack platform and these tools control the key cloud computation tasks, storage, networking, image services, and identity. Multiple optional projects can be assorted to be able to build deployable and distinct cloud environments.

Resources like computing, storage, and memory in virtualization are extracted from various proprietary solutions and diverged using a VM prior to any required distribution. OpenStack makes use of a coherent set of APIs in order to extract the said virtual resources. This eventually leads to detached pools of resources that supply power to standard cloud computing solutions, which are directly used by admins and users for interaction.

OpenStack should not be confused as a virtualization management platform. However, both are stacked higher upon virtualized resources with also being able to locate, report, review, and automate the processes in contrasting vendor environments. However, virtualization management platforms simplify controlling the modifications of the functions and attributes of the virtual resources, while OpenStack wields the virtual resources to execute a blend of tools. Such tools help build a cloud environment as per the five cloud computing criteria stipulated by the *National Institute of Standards and Technology* that include pooled resources, a network, provisioning ability, an UI, and automated resource allotment or controlling.

OpenStack can be described as a string of commands, better referred to as scripts. These scripts are grouped into packages known as projects, which transmit functions that help build the cloud environments. Creation of these environments by OpenStack is based on two primary programs.

- A base OS that executes the commands provided by the OpenStack scripts

- Virtualization, which generates a panel of virtual resources extracted from the hardware

Red Hat OpenStack by itself is not responsible for any resource virtualization; it instead utilizes the resources to develop cloud environments. Similarly, the commands are not executed by OpenStack, it merely transmits them to the base OS. These three components - OpenStack, Virtualization, and base OS - need to be interconnected and work in unison.

Core Elements of OpenStack

Several open source projects contributed to the design of OpenStack architecture. OpenStack uses these projects to set up its *undercloud* and *overcloud*, which are utilized by system administrators and cloud users respectively. *Underclouds* consist of the primary modules required by system administrators to initiate and handle the OpenStack environments of the end users, noted to be *overclouds*.

Six stable key services control the computation, storage, networking, images, and identity apart from the multiple other optional services that differ in developmental fruition. These six key services form the infrastructure that enables the other projects to manage the orchestration, dashboarding, alerting, bare-metal provisioning, controlling, and containerization.

- Nova

- Neutron

- Swift

- Cinder

- Keystone

- Glance

Red Hat OpenStack Platform is bundled in a form that lets users build public, private, or hybrid cloud environments with preexisting hardware. The below-mentioned elements constitute the RHOSP architecture functions:

- Persistent block-level storage

- Entirely distributed block-level storage

- Secure authentication and authorization implementations

- Image storage and VM provisioning engine

- Web interface accessibility to admins and users

- Integrated networking

Figure 4-6 is an advanced illustration of Red Hat OpenStack key services and their interconnectivity.

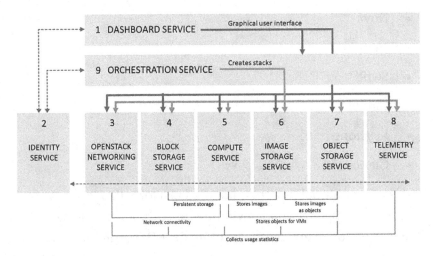

Figure 4-6. *Red Hat OpenStack Core Services*

Dashboard (Code: Horizon)

This is a web-interfaced dashboard that is used for OpenStack services management.

OpenStack Dashboard enables admins and users to operate through a GUI to control functions like generating and spinning up virtual instances, regulating accessibility control, and handling the networking entities.

Admin, Settings, and Projects are the default dashboards included in the Dashboard service. The dashboard can be integrated with other services like monitoring, billing, and other management tools.

Identity (Code: Keystone)

All authentication and authorization of OpenStack services are performed by Keystone. OpenStack Identity enables centralization of its authentication and authorization services for all its units. It is compatible with several authentication techniques like logging credentials, token-oriented systems, and AWS alike login.

OpenStack Networking (Code: Neutron)

Neutron is basically responsible for network interconnectivity over other OpenStack services. Developing and managing virtual networking infrastructure in its cloud is taken care of by OpenStack Networking. The OpenStack managed components of the infrastructure consist of routers, networks, and subnets.

Load-Balancing Service (Code: Octavia)

Load Balancing as a service (LBaaS) is implemented by Octavia to serve the RHOSP director installations. So as to execute load balancing, several provider drivers are made enabled by Octavia. *Amphora* provider driver, which is an open source reference provider driver with high scalability, operates as a reference provider driver performing load balancing. These load-balancing services by the driver are fulfilled by handling a cluster of VMs, together known as *amphorae*, which is spun up as per the requirements.

OpenStack Block Storage (Code: Cinder)

Persistent block storage is enabled by Cinder, and the block storage can be accessed using a self-service API. Persistent block storage management is delivered for virtual HDDs, by OpenStack Block Storage. With the help of Block Storage, users would be able to build and erase block devices and also handle block devices to server connections.

OpenStack Compute (Code: Nova)

Nova is an entire management and accessibility tool dedicated to computational resources like managing the scheduling, developing, and erasure. OpenStack Compute is the key component of OpenStack cloud and provisions VMs as per an on-demand basis. Compute ensures that

VMs are scheduled to be run on a group of nodes through designating the drivers that interconnect with the primary virtualization systems, thus making the features discoverable to the additional OpenStack elements.

OpenStack Image Service (Code: Glance)

Glance is a form of a registry that stores virtual disk images. Storage and recovery of all VM disk images are done by Glance, throughout a wide range of locations. Newer images or snapshots from the current server can be instantly stored in OpenStack Image Service. The snapshots can also be used as a backup or as templates for future server setups.

OpenStack Object Storage (Code: Swift)

Swift is an extremely fault-tolerant object storage service that retains and recovers unorganized data objects through a RESTful API. A storage format for huge data volumes that is accessible by HTTP, it is provisioned by OpenStack Object Storage. The stored data can consist of static units like images, videos, files, VM images, or emails. These objects are saved as binaries on the core file system, while the metadata is saved within the additional aspects of every file.

OpenStack Telemetry (Code: Ceilometer)

The usage data for OpenStack based clouds, at the user level, is delivered by the OpenStack Telemetry. The collected data can be utilized for activities like monitoring of systems, billing, and even alert messages. Telemetry also has the capability to gather data from notifications transmitted by the current OpenStack modules, viz. System usage events, or through recording OpenStack infrastructure resources like *libvirt*.

OpenStack Orchestration (Code: Heat)

OpenStack Orchestration manages the provision of templates, so as to build and maintain the cloud resources like networking, storage, applications, or instances. These templates help build the stacks, which are basically pools of resources.

Red Hat OpenStack Platform Director

The RHOSP director is a toolkit used for the installation and management of an entirely functioning OpenStack environment. With its foundation from the OpenStack project TripleO (OpenStack-On-OpenStack), the project makes use of the OpenStack modules for the installation of an OpenStack environment. It consists of fresh OpenStack elements responsible for provisioning and managing the bare-metal systems that can be operated as OpenStack nodes. This enables an easier way for the RHOSP environment installation.

Scalability with Red Hat Ceph Storage

The Ceph Storage cluster is developed to perform as a distributed data object store that delivers top-notch performance, scalability, and secure dependence. Considered as the future of storage technology, distributed object storage can serve unorganized data and also enable users to operate its latest object interfaces along with the traditional interfaces, concurrently, like the following:

- RESTful interfaces (Swift/S3)

- Filesystem interface

- Multi-language APIs (Java, Python, C/C++)

- Block device interface

Red Hat Ceph Storage holds extreme power to be able to handle enormous volumes of data, specifically for cloud computation such as RHOSP. It is also highly scalable, which facilitates an extensive number of clients with the accessibility of data in petabytes to exabytes, and even further.

The Red Hat Ceph Storage Cluster has three daemon types that are important during deploying Ceph storage.

Ceph OSD Daemon

On account of Ceph clients, Ceph OSDs save the data while also using the memory, networking, and CPU of Ceph nodes so as to carry out the data replication, rebalancing, erasure coding, monitoring, function reporting, and recovery.

Ceph Monitor

The Ceph Monitor is responsible for retaining a master copy of the cluster map of Red Hat Ceph Storage with its existing setup. Peaked coherence is needed by Ceph Monitor while it uses *Paxos* (an algorithm used to resolve network consensus of unreliable processors) to monitor the functioning condition of the Ceph Storage cluster.

Ceph Manager

Data regarding the process and host metadata and placement groups are conserved in a comprehensive manner by the Ceph Manager, as an alternative option to the Ceph Monitor, enhancing the overall functioning. Ceph Manager also controls most of the read-only Ceph CLI queries like placement group statistics. It extends the RESTful monitoring APIs as well.

Data is read from and written to the Red Hat Ceph Storage cluster by interfaces of the Ceph client. The hereunder data is required by clients in order to interact with Red Hat Ceph Storage cluster:

- The configuration file of Ceph, or the monitor address, and the cluster name (mostly *ceph*)

- The pool name

- The username and secret key path

Object IDs and pool names are retained by the Ceph clients, but it is not required by them to retain an object-to-OSD index or establish a communication with a streamlined object index to inquire about object locations. For storage and retrieval purposes, Ceph clients utilize the Ceph Monitor to retrieve the newest Ceph Storage cluster map copy. After that, Ceph clients assign a pool name and object name to librados, which manages the computation of the placement group of an object, and the main OSD to store and retrieve the data through CRUSH (Controlled Replication Under Scalable Hashing) algorithm. A connection is made between the Ceph client and the main OSD, which handles the read/write operations. Among the OSD and client, there is no existence of any mediatory broker, bus, or server.

After data is saved by the OSD, it is supplied with data from a Ceph client, irrespective of the fact that the client might be a Ceph Object Gateway, Ceph Block Device, Ceph Filesystem, or some different interface; the data is stored in the form of an object.

Every data is stored as objects within a flat namespace by the Ceph OSDs. With the absence of any directory hierarchies, a particular object possesses binary data, metadata that includes a name-value pair set, and a unique identifier that is effective clusterwide. The mentioned object identifier is unique not only for the storage media of an OSD but for the whole cluster.

There can be a vast amount of Ceph nodes in a Red Hat Ceph Storage Cluster that allows unbounded scalability, improved availability, and functionality. Every node takes advantage of the hardware that is non-proprietary and acute Ceph daemons that intercommunicate for the following:

- Data integrity assurance

- Failure recovery

- Monitoring and reporting of cluster health also referred to as *heartbeating*

- Durability assurance through replication and coding data erasure

- Dynamic data distribution also referred to as *backfilling*

Hyperconverged Infrastructure Security Best Practices

Numerous organizations are now shifting from legacy infrastructure to hyperconverged infrastructure that will enable them to leverage the consolidated components of the infrastructure, especially in a data center. However, as with other aspects of the IT infrastructure industry, the related security for HCI is often overlooked, which acts as an indirect invitation for cyberattackers. Even if security measures are imposed, it follows strategies that are suitable for the traditional infrastructure and not specific to HCI. Hence it is an absolute necessity to ensure optimum security of the deployed HCI.

Secure Individual Components

There is a misconceived notion that securing an HCI means to deploy security measures for the entire infrastructure unit since all components are consolidated. However, that is not the right way to proceed while implementing security measures for HCI, as securing every individual unit of the infrastructure is more beneficial. And with multiple security layers, you can build an impregnable defense barrier. Despite multiple components being integrated with each other in unison, each unit performs tasks as a separate entity and generates a digital footprint that can be traced back by the attackers and thus expose any underlying vulnerabilities.

Although this was considered inconvenient some time ago, modern tools and technologies have made it comparatively easier to ensure security for each unit. For storage, most vendors offer software-defined encryption that secures both at-rest and in-transit data. With regard to virtualization, Hypervisor vendors now offer fabric protection while shielding for VMs, adding additional security layers. Backup applications with integrated AI have eased the activities for administrators with their capabilities to migrate the backups as per the requirements and perform point-in-time restoration for the infrastructure. These backup applications can also be connected with cloud service providers either by default or through external APIs, which provide supplementary security. Having said all this, it is equally crucial to ensure proper security implementation not only for each separate component but also the entire hyperconverged infrastructure, as an entire unit.

Security Centralization

With modernized developments in HCI, implementing security for data centers in the traditional method is no longer a suitable option. One of the primary advantages of deploying HCI is agility, which is delivered through the elimination of performance constrictions. The traditional security method demands full client installation on every endpoint. Rather than depending on an agent-per-endpoint strategy, this can be overcome by centralizing security and following an agentless strategy. Applying the agentless method will exclude the speed barriers that are intrinsic with full agent-oriented security architecture. By enabling the HCI chassis management platform to provide overall security, the emphasis is transferred from the security agent to the workload performance.

Accessibility

Accessibility for control planes must be minimized for the whole infrastructure since this will restrict any accessibility loopholes and prevent attackers from gaining complete access to HCI clusters.

Security Policies Implementation

Rather than following the traditional approach for implementing a network-based security model, for HCI, it is recommended to apply an application-based security model and policies that will essentially enable the computing instances to intercommunicate over wide network areas. By implementing application-based policies in HCI, infrastructure complexity can be decreased and security can be targeted toward the workloads rather than handling the ports, ACLs, and virtual networks. Every component can be configured to follow specifically curated security policies depicting their individual functionality.

CHAPTER 5

Red Hat Smart Management and Red Hat Insights

This chapter aims to highlight the management of Red Hat Infrastructure across multiple environments and also describe predictive analytics and how it improves the security of any infrastructure.

Serving the world as an infrastructure management solution, Red Hat Satellite assists users for the deployment, configuration, monitoring, and maintenance of multiple systems over the physical, cloud, and virtual environments. Several RHEL systems can be controlled and monitored via this simplified and centralized tool. It is developed specially to cater to the RHEL environments and handle multiple Red Hat Infrastructure components seamlessly with excellent efficiency and security while ensuring compliance with all industry standards.

The Red Hat Satellite Server syncs data from Red Hat services like the Customer Portal along with other sources. It also secures the provision of functions like detailed life-cycle administration; accessibility controls based on group and user role-based models; and access to CLI, GUI, and API, too.

© Rithik Chatterjee 2021
R. Chatterjee, *Red Hat and IT Security*,
https://doi.org/10.1007/978-1-4842-6434-8_5

Red Hat Satellite Architecture

Figure 5-1 provides a detailed overview of the Red Hat Satellite architecture and its phases.

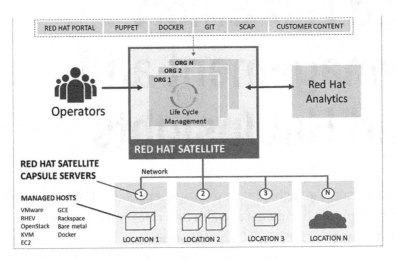

Figure 5-1. *Red Hat Satellite Architecture*

In this architecture data flows through four phases:

1. External Content Sources

   The Satellite Server from Red Hat has the capability to expend varied forms of data through different sources. This is done by maintaining a proper connection with Red Hat Customer Portal that happens to be the main source of errata, software packages, container images and Puppet modules. Supplementary compatible sources like Git repositories, Puppet Forge, SCAP repositories, Docker Hub, or even private organizational data sources can be utilized.

2. Red Hat Satellite Server

    The Red Hat Satellite Server facilitates planning and
    management of the content life cycle along with the
    Capsule Servers and hosts configurations via CLI,
    GUI, and even API. It also administers the life-cycle
    management through making use of organizations in
    the form of principal division units. Organizations are
    responsible for segregating the content for hosts groups
    with particular requirements and administration
    activities. Different teams can use different
    organizations as per their requirements.

    The Red Hat Satellite Server also consists of a thorough
    authentication mechanism that delivers Satellite operators
    with the required access permissions to specialized
    infrastructure components that they are in charge of.

3. Capsule Servers

    Similar to the Satellite Server, Capsule Servers replicate
    data from the Red Hat Satellite Server to set up content
    sources over diverse geographical regions. Data and
    configurations can be fetched by the host machines
    from the Capsule Server in their location itself instead
    of fetching it from the centralized Satellite Server.
    Thus, the suggested least number of Capsule Servers
    is determined based on the amount of geographic
    locations where the Satellite using organization is
    employed. Through the help of Content Views, users
    will be able to define the content subset with accuracy
    that the Capsule Server equips to its hosts. Figure 5-2
    depicts the content life-cycle management using
    Content Views, in Red Hat Satellite.

The connection link shared between the Satellite Server and managed hosts is redirected via the Capsule Server that handles several other services too, on account of these hosts. Services like TFTP, DHCP, DNS, or Puppet Master are delivered by the Capsule Server. A lot of services among these utilize dedicated network ports; however, the Capsule Server makes sure that a sole source IP address is availed for every communication taking place from the host to the Satellite Server. This streamlines the firewall administration as well.

Capsule servers also help users with the scalability of Satellite environments depending upon the increase in systems being handled. This allows the Capsule Server to reduce the resource overhead upon the central server while also improving the bandwidth usage and redundancy.

4. Managed Hosts

Hosts are basically content recipients from Capsule Servers. Virtual hosts are usually deployed on platforms like VMware vSphere, OpenStack, KVM, AWS EC2, Google Cloud Engine, or Rackspace Cloud Services, while physical hosts can also be deployed in private data centers. The Satellite Server may have directly managed hosts, like the base server that runs a Capsule Server can be considered as a managed host of the Satellite Server.

Figure 5-2 illustrates a detailed overview of content distribution from the Satellite Server to Capsules.

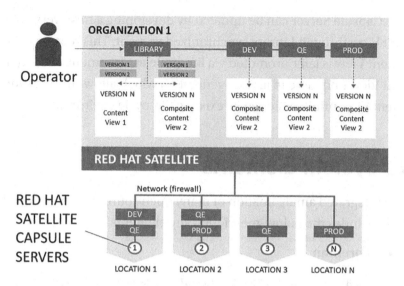

Figure 5-2. *Red Hat Satellite Content Life Cycle*

Every organization has a content Library by default, derived from other sources. Content Views are nothing more than subsets of the content from the Library generated by intelligent filtering. Content Views can be published and promoted to SDLC environments. During the creation of a Capsule Server, the chosen life-cycle environment is replicated to the particular Capsule while provisioning its availability to the managed hosts.

Through merging, Composite Content Views can also be developed. Having a different Content View for a package repository can be useful, as one is needed by an OS and another package repository is needed by an application. Any packages updates in a repository just need reissuing of the applicable Content View. The Composite Content Views can then be utilized for the merging of Content Views that are published. Based on the intended operation of the Capsule, the promotion of any Content Views to a particular Capsule Server is decided.

The Capsule Server can be updated by developing a fresh versioned Content View through Library synchronized content. This recent version of Content View is later promoted via life-cycle environments. On-spot Content View updates can also be generated, which allows the creation of a Content View mini-version in its existing life-cycle environment.

Core System Elements

With an integrated amalgamation of many open source solutions, Red Hat Satellite includes the below-mentioned key elements.

- **Foreman**

  As an open source tool, *Foreman* assists with provisioning and handling the life cycle of virtual and physical systems. *Foreman* performs automated system configuration through different ways such as Kickstart and Puppet modules. It also yields historical data that is used for troubleshooting, auditing, and reporting.

- **Katello**

  Katello is basically a *Foreman* extension that handles the repository and subscription management. It is like a mediator that helps users with the subscription of Red Hat repositories and download content. Various versions of this content can be generated and handled while deploying them on any systems in user-specified phases of the software life cycle.

- **Candlepin**

  Candlepin is a *Katello* service that takes care of subscription management.

- **Pulp**

  Pulp is also a *Katello* service that controls content and
  repository management. *Pulp* organizes the storage
  space systematically, by not replicating any RPM
  packages, despite being asked for them by Content
  Views in various organizations.

- **Hammer**

  As a CLI tool, *Hammer* enables users with shell and
  command-line operations that are analogous with the
  majority of Web UI functionality.

- **REST API**

  A RESTful API service is part of Red Hat Satellite that
  enables system admins and the development team
  to develop customized scripts and integrate external
  applications with Satellite.

Organizations

Resources in Red Hat Satellite are split into logical groups by
Organizations. Depending upon the ownership, content, security level,
purpose, or some different divisions, the resources are split. Several
Organizations can be built and handled using Satellite, which also takes
care of dividing and assigning Red Hat subscriptions to every individual
Organization. This way, the content of many separate Organizations can be
efficiently managed through a single management system.

Locations

Locations are responsible for splitting Organizations into logical groups
depending on geographic regions. Every Location is utilized by a sole Red
Hat customer account, but per account is able to handle many Locations
and Organizations.

Red Hat Satellite adopts a unified procedure to handle Location and Organization Management. Numerous Locations and Organizations in a sole Satellite Server are defined by system admins. For instance, an enterprise with three Organizations: Engineering, Operations, and Accounts, spread out over three geographic Locations: Asia, America, and Europe, the Satellite Server here would handle all three Organizations over the three Locations, thus producing nine distinct system management contexts. Additionally, Locations can be specifically user defined so as to nest them into a hierarchy development.

Every Organization and Location is defined by the Satellite Server. Content is synchronized and system configurations at various Locations are managed by each corresponding Satellite Capsule Server.

The primary Satellite Server preserves the management functions, during which configuration and content synchronization take place between a regionally allocated Satellite Capsule Server and the primary Satellite Server.

Life-Cycle Environments

Software life cycles are split into life-cycle environments, representing every phase of the software life cycle. Life-cycle environments are connected to develop an environment path. Content across the environment path can be promoted to the upcoming life-cycle environment as per the requirement. For example, if development concludes on a specific software version, this version can then be promoted to the testing environment while commencing development on the following version.

Provisioning

One of the key functionalities of Red Hat Satellite is unattended host provisioning. In order to execute it, DHCP and DNS infrastructures, TFTP, Kickstart, and PXE booting are utilized by Satellite.

Kickstart

Kickstart is used for an automated installation procedure of Red Hat Satellite and Capsule Server. This is done by generating a Kickstart file consisting of the entire installation information that will be needed.

Upon execution of a Kickstart script, the workflow occurs in the following manner:

- The installation location of a Capsule Server and Satellite Server is defined.

- Predefined packages are installed.

- Red Hat Subscription Manager is installed.

- Activation Keys are used for host subscriptions to Red Hat Satellite.

- Puppet is installed and configured with a puppet.conf file for an indication of Capsule instance or Red Hat Satellite.

- Puppet is enabled for execution and then creates a request for a certificate.

- User-specified snippets are executed.

PXE Booting

PXE (Preboot Execution Environment) facilitates the feature of a system boot over a network. Rather than utilizing the usual storage drives, PXE operates via DHCP so as to deliver standard information to hosts regarding the network, to locate a TFTP server, and to download a boot image as well.

The PXE workflow occurs in the following sequence:

- The PXE image is booted by the host after resulting as the only boot image being found.

- A broadcast request is sent to the DHCP server by a host NIC.

- After receiving the request, the DHCP server transmits standard information regarding the network like IP address, gateway, subnet mask, TFTP server location, boot image, and DNS.

- The bootloader `image/pxelinux.0` along with the configuration file `pxelinux.cfg/00:MA:CA:AD:D` is obtained by the host from the TFTP server.

- The location of the kernel image, `initrd,` and Kickstart is defined by the host configuration.

- The files are later downloaded and the image is installed by the host.

Red Hat Satellite facilitates deployment in multiple methods as per user requirements. A few of such deployment scenarios are mentioned below.

Single Location

Through the course of the installation procedure, an integrated Capsule Server (a virtual Capsule Server) is produced by default in the Satellite Server. This means that Satellite Server can be utilized for provisioning of directly connected hosts to deploy the Satellite Server in a sole geographic region; hence there is a requirement of just one physical server. The Satellite Server can promptly handle the base systems of isolated Capsules, but using this method to handle different hosts located remotely is neither ideal nor advised.

Single Location with Separate Subnets

Despite deploying Red Hat Satellite in one geographic region, a particular infrastructure may need many separated or detached subnets. This can be executed by multiple Capsule Server deployments running with DNS and DHCP services; however, it is advisable to generate separate subnets through the same Capsule. Computing resources and hosts in the separated networks are handled by that Capsule Server. It is done to make sure that the hosts and resources are able to access the Capsule just for configuration, provisioning, general management, and errata.

Multiple Locations

Ideally, it is better to create a minimum of a single Capsule Server for each geographic region. This method can conserve bandwidth as hosts fetch content out of a local Capsule Server. Instead of each host in a location, it is just the Capsule that synchronizes the content from remote repositories. Additionally, through this layout, the provisioning infrastructure offers a simplistic and reliable configuration.

Disconnected Satellite

For highly secure environments, hosts are often needed to operate in an isolated network without an internet connection. Red Hat Satellite usually provides the systems with new security patch updates, packages, and errata among other required content; but despite being disconnected from the internet, Red Hat Satellite does not let the other infrastructure systems get affected. Even a disconnected Satellite Server can import content in either of two ways, both of which can also be utilized to hasten a connected Satellite's inceptive population.

Disconnected Satellite with Content ISO

In this configuration, ISO images are downloaded with content from the Red Hat Customer Portal and are acquired and redirected to the Satellite Server or some local web server. Post that, there is a local synchronization of the Satellite Server content. This enables a totally isolated network for the Satellite Server but the content ISO images have a release period of six weeks apart, with the exclusion of many solution contents. Details regarding this can be verified through the Customer Portal.

Disconnected Satellite with Inter-Satellite Synchronization

In this configuration, initially, a connected Satellite Server is installed and then its content is migrated for populating a disconnected Satellite via a storage drive. By following this method, both Red Hat content, as well as custom content, can be exported at a user-chosen frequency. The only catch is that this execution needs a supplementary server with a different subscription.

Capsule with External Services

A Capsule Server, whether a stand-alone or an integrated one, can be configured for using external DNS, TFTP, or DHCP service. Satellite Servers with preexisting external services in an environment can be integrated with a Satellite deployment.

Infrastructure Controlling with Red Hat Smart Management

Organizations are gradually drifting apart from legacy infrastructure and adopting hybrid or multi-cloud infrastructures. Handling the administration and operations of these environments can be a daunting task, considering all the complexity associated with it. This causes users to deal with issues like the following:

- Making sure that all the systems are regularly updated and provide scalability.

- Juggle with the required flexibility to handle on-premise and cloud environments simultaneously.

- Maintaining compliance with industrial standards and regulations.

- Constant monitoring, analyzing, and troubleshooting of potential security threats and vulnerabilities.

To improve the complex issues and tackle such challenges while managing Red Hat infrastructure, Red Hat Smart Management has been developed. It is useful for management and optimization of RHEL environments in multiple systems. Users are provided with options to handle RHEL in their preferred environment: on-premise or cloud. It is done just through a sole subscription that focuses on the primary issues related to compliance, security, patching, and provisioning. Smart Management can control the complete infrastructure system and security management life cycle.

Red Hat Smart Management consists of Red Hat Satellite, modern cloud management services for RHEL, and Red Hat Insights (that we will be discussing later on in this chapter). Red Hat Satellite, a platform that provides immense scalability, is one of the main components of Red Hat Smart Management. Satellite handles all the provisioning, subscriptions, and patching of the Red Hat infrastructure systems.

Another component of Smart Management is RHEL cloud management services that is a SaaS feature. Using this, users can select their RHEL management method: on-prem or cloud solution. The cloud management services comprise compliance, system comparison, and vulnerability, all of which are hosted on *cloud.redhat.com*. If users require a legacy management solution for their on-prem RHEL environment, then it can be done so using Red Hat Satellite. However, if users require a cloud-oriented hosted management solution, they can select the cloud management services for RHEL. During a few situations, there may also be the demand for managing certain environment elements on-prem while handling other environment elements through a cloud management solution.

As the RHEL cloud management solution is completely cloud oriented, the need for any infrastructure installation or maintenance is eliminated. Also, Red Hat ensures that it will verify the operations and features of the latest version that is run on user systems, so as to prevent any downtimes. In order to connect the hosts to the RHEL cloud management services, every host must have Insights client installed in it.

The cloud management services include the following services:

- Vulnerability management for monitoring, evaluating, reporting, and resolving CVEs.

- Compliance management for monitoring, evaluating, reporting, and resolving security compliance regulations.

- System Comparison for differentiating the variations among multiple systems and then reporting them.

One of the key aspects of Red Hat Smart Management is its Cloud Connector that delivers efficient remediation of all the risks that have been identified through the dashboard of Red Hat Insights. In this process, Smart Management is also assisted by Red Hat Satellite for remediating the identified risks and managing the infrastructure as well.

Predictive Analytics Using Red Hat Insights

With increasing complexity in infrastructure environments, at times, admins have to verify the basic system checks like network or server settings for troubleshooting and even standard routine tasks, before moving onto advanced verifications like kernel updates, *Meltdown* and *Spectre* (advanced vulnerability variations infecting computer chips) checks, and so on. These tedious system activities can be carried out by Red Hat Insights, which can not only discover the issues but also figure out its resolutions. If integrated with Ansible playbooks, the process of troubleshooting and issue remediations can be automated.

Serving as a SaaS, Red Hat Insights consistently and extensively analyzes Red Hat products and solutions, to dynamically discover threats and vulnerabilities related to availability, stability, performance, and security, over virtual, physical, and cloud infrastructures. The base of Insights utilizes an artificially intelligent rules engine that compares system configuration data with predefined rules, so as to discover technical issues that have arisen.

Figure 5-3 represents the basic architecture of Red Hat Insights. Content from the infrastructure undergoes a server data anonymization with minimal impact on the network and later delivered to Red Hat Satellite and Red Hat CloudForms. The alerts and results from Insights can be viewed from either the Customer Portal or the Satellite UI. The results are customized for each host that includes the remediation process and the Ansible playbooks as well.

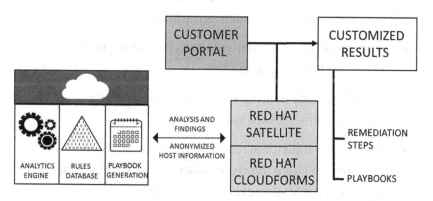

Figure 5-3. *Red Hat Insights Architecture*

Red Hat Insights include Policies services that enable users to specify custom internal policies and accordingly receive notifications based on any environment misalignments. Another security functionality is the Patch service that performs analysis of the Red Hat product advisories, applicable to the RHEL systems, keeping them updated. Additional services include Compliance, Drift, and Vulnerability services, all of which when merged, deliver an extensive RHEL management solution.

Advisor Service

The advisor service in Insights can be used for evaluating and monitoring the condition or robustness of a RHEL infrastructure. It can be in case of isolated or connected systems, or even the entire infrastructure, that configuration issues might cause hindrance to stability, availability, functionality, and especially the security of the environment. The advisor service assists users in resolving such configuration issues.

Post the installation and registration of the Insights client on a system, the client application self-executes against a Recommendations (previously called rules) database. These can be classified as sets of conditions that could expose the RHEL systems to risks. After the completion of this step, data is later uploaded to the Recommendations page in the advisor service, allowing users to execute actions such as the following:

- Observe all the Recommendations pertaining to the complete RHEL infrastructure.

- Utilizing sturdy filtering service for processing the views to more relevant systems.

- Identify the individual recommendations with information about the risks associated with them, and remediations for those individual systems.

- Sharing of results with management and other teams.

- Creating and handling the Ansible playbooks for remediations enabling to resolve the issues through the Insights application.

Each recommendation consists of the below-mentioned supplementary information:

- Description (Name)

  Brief details about the recommendation.

- Date published

  Date of the recommendation publication in the Advisor service archive.

- Knowledgebase articles

  Red Hat link to find out more information about the issue.

- Total risk

  A derived value from the possibility of a condition inversely affecting an environment along with the impact it would have on the system functionality, it was to actually occur.

- Risk of change

  The involved operations risk associated with the resolution being implemented.

- Reboot required

  Whether or not a system reboot would be needed, which might further lead to downtime.

- Affected systems

  The list of systems that the recommendations are detected and based on.

During the prevalence of a recommendation in a system, the Insights Advisor service provides in-depth information about the effect that a recommendation is having on a particular system, especially regarding its emergence and remediation. Users can observe this data while viewing a recommendation and specifying a system that is affected.

Descriptive tags can be added to the systems that are handled by Insights, which will enable users to link contextual markers to each system. The systems can later be filtered in the Insights application using those tags, helping locate different or similar systems. This characteristic is crucial during the deployment of Insights on a larger scale, handled by Insights management.

Tags include a pair of namespace/key=value structure.

- Namespace

    It is the permanent name given to the ingestion point, insights-client. Derived from the namespace, the tags. yaml file is extracted and injected by the client before an upload.

- Key

    The key can either be system specified or user customized. A blend of letters, capitalization, symbols, numbers, or even whitespace, can be used.

- Value

    Users are allowed to define their own descriptive string value. Similar to a key, multiple character combinations can be used to define it.

User customized tags are provided in the /etc/insights-client/ tags.yaml file. Numerous key-value pairs could be added to the tags.yaml file, as per the requirements. The configuration tends to be easier to alter because of the YAML syntax.

Executing the `insights-client --group=eastern-sap` generates the configuration file for tags: `/etc/insights-client/tags.yaml` along with registering group: `eastern-sap`. The below-mentioned YAML script of a `tags.yaml` file has supplemental tags added for the eastern-sap group.

```
# tags
---
group: eastern-sap
name: Diana Prince
contact: dprince@xyz.com
Zone: eastern time zone
Location:
- black_rack
- basement
Application: SAP
```

Vulnerability Service

One of the major service offerings by Red Hat Insights is the Vulnerability service. It effectively assesses and monitors any exposures in the RHEL systems with respect to the CVEs (Common Vulnerabilities and Exposures) database. This will allow users to gain a better understanding of the underlying critical issues while the service also assists to figure out its resolution.

Your data is shared with the Vulnerability service, and as a user you will be able to sort and filter system groups and CVEs that will help with your view optimization. Custom contexts can also be included with individual CVEs if you discern that a vulnerability carries a high-risk factor. With better knowledge about the risk exposures, you could also build Ansible playbooks that will resolve the issues in an automated fashion, providing efficiency and optimum security to the environments.

CVEs can be described as security vulnerabilities discovered in publicly released application packages. These CVEs are listed in the database that is recognized by the *National Cybersecurity FFRDC (NCF)*.

Security Rules

Red Hat CVEs are the security rules that have been priorly recognized by the Red Hat Insights application. These deserve more visibility because of the risks, vulnerabilities, and exposures linked to them.

The Red Hat Product Security team utilizes the Customer Security Awareness (CSAw) Program workflow, for a manual creation of algorithms that assists with the RHEL environment exposure of the users, allowing them to take necessary steps to safeguard their organization. If any single or even multiple systems are discovered as an exposure to a security rule, they will be potentially vulnerable to security threats and all issues pertaining to it would require immediate attention.

Not necessarily every system that is exposed to a particular CVE will also be exposed to any security rule that is linked to that CVE. Also, any given Red Hat CVE might have more than one security rule linked to it, while the contrary also holds true.

Users can determine the business risk of a CVE with the help of the Vulnerability service. The risk criteria are High, Medium, Low, or Not Defined (default). The CVEs list displays the severity of each business risk, but specifying the risks enables users to determine an order of the CVEs depending upon the potential impact they might have on an organization. Through this, additional control is provided to the users, allowing them to effectively handle the risks, especially in bigger environments.

Compliance Service

The Compliance service is responsible for evaluating and monitoring the RHEL systems for compliance with SCAP (Security Content Automation Protocol) security regulations.

With a minimal yet efficient UI, the Compliance service enables users for building, configuring, and handling the SCAP policies, right in the Compliance service. The service includes default features of context-adding and filtering, which provide uncomplicated compliance issue identification and management. Prior to using the Compliance service, as a user, you will need to ensure that:

- Insights client is installed and registered on every system that needs to be monitored.

- Configuration of OpenSCAP with datastreams and SCAP security guides (SSGs) to be able to perform data reporting to the Compliance service. Later on, the policies can be amended through the service.

No matter which method you prefer while specifying the policies, among the options of defining policy in Compliance directly or uploading policy reports that are managed and defined external of the Compliance service, just the SSG version that is shipped with the mini-version of installed RHEL on systems will be completely supported and compatible by the Compliance service.

As every SSG version varies from the earlier version, precise reporting can be performed only by employing the set of rules that the proper SSG version for RHEL consists of. The application also recognizes the systems installed with incompatible SCAP versions.

In order to use the Compliance service, the SCAP security policies need to be linked with the RHEL systems. A new policy can be created through the Compliance service wizard that consist of the below-mentioned actions.

- Identifying the host OS

- Choosing a policy

- Modifying the predefined rules

- Connecting systems to the policy

All reports included in the Compliance service are organized by SSG (SCAP Security Guide) version. In case several SSG versions have been deployed on systems that are allocated to a particular policy, one report per SSG version will be visible to the users.

In order to create a fresh policy and link systems to it through the Compliance service, the following actions will have to be performed.

- Go to the Compliance service ➤ SCAP Policies page (log in if required).

- Select Create new policy option and proceed to the Create SCAP policy wizard.

- In the Create SCAP policy page, choose the proper RHEL OS version ➤ select type of policy ➤ select next.

- After proceeding to the Policy details page, review or edit the data in the fields.

- On the same page, provide a Policy Name ➤ Reference ID will remain unchanged ➤ edit or continue with the OpenSCAP description ➤ provide a system Compliance threshold ➤ select next.

- The policy can be edited by adding or erasing rules, in the Rules page ➤ select next.

- After proceeding to the Systems page, select the systems that have to be linked with this policy ➤ select next.

- Verify the policy information in the Review page ➤ select finish.

The Compliance service uses a technique called the compliance threshold, which determines the percentage of rules that needs to be passed to ensure the compliance of a system. The default value is 100% that can be modified during the creation of a policy or later on as well, depending on preference. After having configured the threshold value, it can be viewed in the policies list.

Considering every pairing of a rule and a system, the process to remediate the issue is provided by the Compliance service, while it also delivers automated remediation with the help of Ansible playbooks.

The strategies mentioned below are followed by the Compliance service to resolve the issues:

- Remediating more than one system and applying a single policy so as to calibrate and make the policy gain an acceptable compliance threshold.

- Remediating several rules, regardless of the number of policies, which affect the compliance status of a sole system.

System Comparison / Drift Analysis

The System Comparison service allows the users to be able to differentiate the configuration of a system with another system in an inventory of cloud management services. The system configurations can also be tracked and compared through time for analyzing any modifications. For better efficiency, a reference point can be set, so that all the systems can be further compared to that reference point. Such comparisons can be used to troubleshoot system issues that will also help to determine the cause of those issues and how to prevent them in the future.

Using the UI to compare various systems, users will be able to filter and display profile facts that are virtually the same, similar, different, or even data that is missing. It is also possible to manage and define baselines (elaborated later on in this topic) through this service. After defining the baselines, it can be used in System Comparison for comparing baselines along with the system configurations. After the process, a CSV output with all the details of the system and baseline comparisons can be produced.

The Drift Analysis or the System Comparison tool utilizes the insights-client so there is no need for any additional tool for installation. Users can directly compare the systems that are registered in the cloud management services inventory, regardless of whether the systems are hosted on physical infrastructure, private cloud, or even public cloud environments.

System profiles and RHEL configurations can be examined by using Insights. Having the Drift service, system profiles can be selected and viewed throughout time while being able to avail them in the comparisons. With profile analysis, users can learn more about system characteristics, like the following:

- System hardware and modifications related to it

- System configuration modifications that might have taken place

- Installed updates that have to be validated

- Operational issues that would require troubleshooting

Whenever a system is submitted to be compared, the profile is checked by the submission while marking it with a timestamp. Because of performing analysis of multiple profile versions, users can get to observe the system view throughout time.

Through Drift Analysis, differences in system configurations can be identified and analyzed that will help determine the root cause of a particular change in the configuration. This proves to be beneficial when a rogue application or threat covertly manages to alter system settings for further exploitation. When such threats spread throughout multiple systems, it becomes very difficult for system administrators to troubleshoot and figure out the source of origin of the threat, contain it, and implement appropriate security remediations.

System Baselines

Baselines can be described as configurations specifiable from ground zero, in the form of a replica of a current system configuration or another baseline. After being defined, baselines can be utilized through the System Comparison service that will help compare system configurations and baselines, while handling the system profile definitions for an organization. A baseline can also be altered by means of modifying fact values or erasing them.

There are three basic options available to generate a baseline:

- Creating a baseline from scratch

- Copying a current baseline

- Copying a current system

Baselines are extremely useful when a particular set of configurations have to be used as a comparison standard for other/future system configurations. These should not be confused with a reference point as Baselines can be freshly created and also modified as per requirements.

Reference Point

Based on requirements, every system might often be needed to be compared to a sole reference point, instead of comparing every system among each other or even a group. Like, the systems might be required to be compared with a baseline in order to calculate all the systems against it. Timestamps can also be used for systems to be compared against, which will provide better insight into all the occurred changes and assist with the troubleshooting of any accidental, unauthorized, or malicious system configuration changes.

Comparisons can also be reversed, such as rather than comparing older timestamped system profiles against a new profile, it might be better to compare every profile against a system's oldest available operational version. Through a comparison like that, changes varying from the reference point can be easier to distinguish.

System Facts

The baselines and system configurations are defined by a set of system facts. These system facts are pair properties of name and value, consisting of configuration entities attributes, like system packages and network interface settings. System facts can be accessed, used, and filtered, as a component of baseline comparison and system configuration.

The state of the comparison depending on noted fact values imparts information about the system management. Facts that have different behavior than expected are flagged by the application before identifying facts with an unknown state and notifying users about the facts that might be problematic and worth heeding. This helps in identifying any abnormal anomalies/patterns that usually occur when an application or system is compromised and a threat tries to exploit unpatched vulnerabilities.

Insights Policies

The system configurations in an environment are assessed by Policies before they are processed upon receiving the upload of an insights-client workload to *cloud.redhat.com*. Depending on whether single or multiple conditions are satisfied, predefined actions are activated. All Insights inventory registered systems are employed with policies, which can be created and handled through the UI or API.

174

Webhooks

Policies can be integrated with webhooks for Insights, based on the required actions. The webhooks send POST alerts to notify external applications compatible with webhooks integration. Through this, users are provided with the flexibility to integrate *cloud.redhat.com* into their default functional workflow. Hooks can also be used by integrating with policies; whenever a certain event or condition is fulfilled, the trigger action can be set as send to hook (third-party application).

System Patching Using Ansible Playbooks

Through the use of Red Hat Software and Management automation, Patching provides seamless patch workflows for RHEL components over an open hybrid cloud environment. This delivers a canonical perspective of relevant advisories over all the deployments, be it the public cloud, hosted Red Hat Subscription Management, or Red Hat Satellite.

Patching would enable users to perform the following:

- Observing all the relevant Red Hat advisories for the RHEL components part of the Insights.

- Utilizing single or multiple advisories with Ansible playbooks for patching of any system, through Remediations.

If Red Hat Insights is integrated with Smart Management, the relevant risks associated with an operation can be highlighted and resolved, even on a large scale. Due to this, the operations and security risk management can be streamlined with minimal manual intervention.

CHAPTER 6

Red Hat Security Auditing

This chapter aims to highlight the processes related to IT security auditing, its best practices, and auditing implementations in RHEL systems.

IT System Auditing

Information systems audit, also known as IT audit, can be defined as the systematic and independent evaluation of the IT infrastructure, operations, and policies of an organization. These may include management controls, data processing systems, storage and networking systems, accessibility controls, security policies, and all the interfaces associated with these systems. Information system audits are essential to accomplish the objectives and verify the compliance of policies charted out by an organization. Auditing not only validates the individual system elements that help achieve the predefined objectives, but it also generates valid evidence that emphasizes on lowering, elimination, and avoidance of non-conformities.

Organizing an IT audit consists of two stages: the initial stage is Footprinting or Reconnaissance that is basically information gathering and planning accordingly; the second stage is to comprehend the current internal operating infrastructure. Organizations also prefer performing risk-based auditing, which assesses the involved risks, depending on

© Rithik Chatterjee 2021
R. Chatterjee, *Red Hat and IT Security*,
https://doi.org/10.1007/978-1-4842-6434-8_6

which the auditor discerns the need for substantive testing or compliance testing. The risk-based auditing makes the auditors rely more on the operational and internal controls. This proves beneficial for organizations to correlate the cost-benefit analysis to the risks associated with the controls. The fingerprinting stage includes five primary constituents for information gathering:

- Fundamental risk assessments

- Regulatory statutes

- Previous year's audit reports

- Latest financial data

- Industry and business knowledge

IT audits do not just entail the evaluation of the physical security controls, it also includes examining the financial and business controls relevant to the IT systems. The key objectives of an IT audit are the following:

- Evaluation of the IT systems and processes that secure the organization's data.

- Determine the efficacy of system implementations in fulfilling the predefined objectives of an organization.

- Verify the compliance of information management systems with standard IT policies and regulations.

- Analyze and ascertain the risks associated to the data assets of an organization and provide assistance in resolving and preventing those risks.

- Deduce the inefficiencies and non-conformities in systems, processes, controls, and administration related to IT.

One of the major IT audit strategies includes deciding to choose between compliance testing and substantive testing. Compliance testing includes information gathering to ensure the conformities while substantive testing consists of information gathering for evaluating the data integrity and identifying possible fraud like a material misstatement, invalid documentation. and so on. Both types of testing can be better described in the following scenario.

In case of compliance testing, suppose an organization mandates for all network changes to follow change control. Based on this, an IT auditor may tally the latest network configuration with the recent previous version of the configuration file of the network, compare and highlight the differences, and later verify them in accordance with the supposed change control documentation. IT administrators often fail to follow the changes as per the change control.

In substantive testing, suppose an organization has a backup policy to store at least the latest five versions of a backup in a cloud repository. An IT auditor would check and compare the stored backup versions with the locally available versions along with ensuring that all five versions are properly stored.

General Controls vs. Application Controls

General controls are applied to almost every aspect of an organization related to the IT infrastructure and its services. Mentioned below are a few such controls:

- Operative controls

- Administration controls

- Private accounting controls

- Security policies and procedures of an organization

- Logical and physical security guidelines encompassing all IT resources and environments

- Systems and implementations to facilitate efficient security measures concerning accessibility

- Standard policies governing design and usage of appropriate documentation and records

Meanwhile, application controls are pertinent to the data and transactions associated with every individual computer-oriented application system, which makes them distinct to every application. Application controls are IPO (Input, Processing, Output) function controls that are required to ascertain the thoroughness and validity of the records and the entries made within them. The controls consist of practices to verify:

- Data entered and updated in the system are entirely valid, precise, and complete

- Data maintenance

- Data processing achieves the defined and proper task

- The results of the processing are met with the actual expectations

- Critical data is safe and encrypted

- Credential system

Apart from compliance and substantive audit approaches mentioned above, there are several other forms of system audits with specific requirements and use cases.

- Adequacy Audit

  This type of audit is conducted to verify the compliance of policy documentation, codes of guidelines, procedures, and practices as per the standard rules and regulations. This results in deciding whether these policy and procedure systems comply with the standard norms and if these provide the required objective evidence of a well-designed system.

- External Audit

  Also referred to as a second-party audit, this audit is performed by consultants or organizations operating externally and with whom there is no agreement to acquire any products or services in any way. An external audit can include either compliance or adequacy audit, or both.

- Extrinsic Audit

  Also referred to as a third-party audit, this audit is performed by an accredited autonomous individual or organization that uses a standard to deliver assurance regarding the system efficiency. The audit can be adequacy or compliance audit, or both.

- Internal Audit

  This type of audit, which is also known as a first-party audit, is conducted by an organization internally through its own systems and resources, so as to assure the management about the well-functioning systems and successfully achieving of the predefined objectives. The audit is conducted by organization members that are not directly related to the system. Organizations often also employ exterior consultants with expertise to help conduct such internal audits.

- Process Audit

  This is a vertical audit that covers the entire system involved in the development workflow of a particular product or service to be provided to end users. This audit evaluates and decides whether the processes, resources, and activities involved are being operated with the required efficiency and standards.

Risk Analysis

A risk can be termed as the likelihood of losing something valuable. The process of risk analysis is initiated with the phase of planning to secure the systems after discovering the system vulnerabilities and the impact they would have. Post that, a strategy is devised to handle the risks, remediate them, and subsist a critical event. The last part is included to access the odds of a cyber disaster followed by its economic damage.

Risk analysis includes the following primary steps:

- Identifying all the units connected to the system that are part of the audit scope

- Identifying all threats and issues associated with all the system components

- Risk quantification (assessing the loss when/if threats truly occur)

Figure 6-1 illustrates that the first step in risk analysis is identifying the hazards and then analyzing the hazard and scenarios. Later, the likelihood of a scenario with that hazard and the consequences it would have are considered. Based on all these factors, the risk is calculated and the overall process of risk analysis is performed.

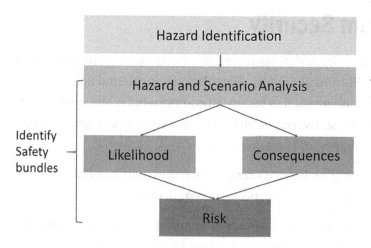

Figure 6-1. *Risk Analysis Flowchart*

Threats and risks are constantly evolving, which also changes the inherent loss to be incurred. Hence the risk management practices and procedures must also be adaptive and be conducted on a frequent basis.

Risk management includes the following actions:

- Security measure identification

- Estimating the capital investment required for the execution of the security measures

- Differentiating between the security measures costs and threat possibilities with losses to be incurred

- Determining the most appropriate security measures to be implemented

- Security measures assessment

System Security

System security addresses protecting the system against unauthorized accessibility and alterations, data theft, or accidental data losses. In system security, it is essential to secure all components of the system that consists of hardware, software, and data. The two key units of system security are system integrity and system privacy.

- System integrity covers the nature and reliability of both raw and processed system data.

- System privacy refers to securing all relevant systems to prevent unapproved access from individuals or through any applications. System data should not be shared or compromised without the consent of the concerning individual or organization.

Control Objectives and Environment

In the footprinting phase that includes preliminary accumulating data, the auditor is able to verify the scope of the audit along with forming control objectives, to be used for the audit testing. Control objectives are basically management practices that are instituted to maintain the required system controls, essential for the audit objective. It is highly prioritized during the audits to ensure the practices are actively followed by the management and eventually achieve the preset control objectives. The *Control Environment* also known as *Internal Control Environment*, is the overall processes, standards, culture, structure, and policies set by the management that act as the foundation for the internal control system of an organization.

Finding

When no evidence can be observed that corresponds with a provided control objective, the issue will be termed as a *finding* by the auditor. Documented audits consist of four to five parts:

- Condition

  An accurate evidence description derived from the audit.

- Criteria

  Predefined standards that signify the reason behind the condition impeding the management ability to attain the control objectives.

- Cause

  The main cause of the circumstances leading to ineffective controls.

- Effect

  The inherent risk posed by the condition to the organization mentioned, referring to the potential business impact.

- Recommendation

  A suitable response that can be undertaken by the management.

Best Practices for Red Hat System Audit

An audit is not meant for provisioning enhanced security for a system or environment. Its main purpose is to identify the violations and conformities of the security procedures and policies, governing the systems. Red Hat Linux offers the primordial security measures for the systems through SELinux.

The auditing system in Linux allows us to track the security-related system data. Depending on predefined rules, log entries are generated by the audit process that records critical data regarding all the events occurring in the system. The recorded data proves to be quite beneficial, especially for imperative environments that help decide the nonconformist and their actions with respect to the preset security practices and policies.

Some of the key information that is recorded during the Audit in the log files are mentioned below.

- Date, time, type, and result of an event

- Subject and object sensitivity levels

- Correlating an event with the identity of the user responsible for triggering the said event

- Access attempts to the log files of the audit

- Every alteration to the audit configuration

- Authentication mechanisms use cases like Kerberos, SSH, among more

- Modifying a particular trusted database like */etc/passwd*

- Attempts to exchange information to and from the system

- Including and excluding events depending on subject/object labels, user identity, and other aspects as well

RHEL Audit Use Cases

Below are some audit use cases:

- System Call Monitoring

  With proper audit configuration, for every specific
  system call execution, a log entry will be generated.
  This is applicable in situations like tracking
  modifications in system time, through monitoring of
  settimeofday, clock_adjtime, and further time-based
  system calls.

- Observing File Access

  Directories that have been accessed, executed, or
  amended, or even if the attributes of the file are
  changed, it can be tracked via Audit. It can be helpful
  like when users need to identify the access to critical
  files with just the audit trail at disposal, largely if any of
  the files turn out to be corrupted.

- Recording Executed Commands

  The audit has the ability to track file executions;
  thus by defining rules all the executions of a specific
  command can also be tracked. For each executable
  located in the /bin directory, a rule can be defined.
  Whatever log entries are produced as a result, through
  user ID filtration, an audit trail can be created of all the
  commands that are executed by each user.

- Recording processing of system pathnames

  Apart from the process of routing a path to an inode
  during invoking a rule, available in file access
  observation, Audit can also keep a track of the path

execution, regardless of whether it is present at the rule invocation or if the file is restored after that. Because of this, rules are enabled to provide consistent execution prior to an installation of a program executable or even post its upgrade.

- Recording Security Events

  Unsuccessful login attempts can be recorded by the `pam_faillock` authentication module. By configuring the audit, along with failed login attempts, more information regarding the user that tried to log in can also be recorded.

- Processing Summary Reports

  Tasks like daily reports of recorded events and so on can be produced by the `aureport` utility. The reports can then be evaluated and investigated by system admins to identify any suspicious activity.

- Event Searching

  The log entries can be filtered to produce an audit trail in its entirety, depending on various conditions, all through the help of the `ausearch` utility provisioned by Audit.

- Network Access Monitoring

  System admins can monitor the network access by configuring the `iptables` and `ebtables` utilities that trigger Audit events.

Audit System Architecture

The audit system is comprised of two key elements:

- Kernel-side system call processing

- User-space applications and utilities

System calls are received by the kernel-side system from the user-space applications, and the system calls are then filtered through any of these filters: *task, user, fstype*, or *exit*.

After a system call is processed via the *exclude* filter, it is routed through any of the filters specified above. Depending on the configuration of the audit rule, it is later sent to the Audit daemon for extended processing. The process is represented in Figure 6-2 provided below.

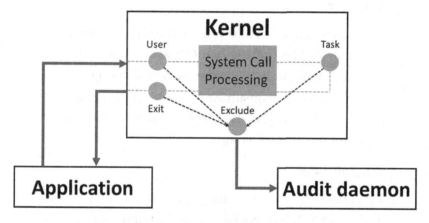

Figure 6-2. *System Call Processing Filtration*

Data is gathered from the kernel to generate log file entries by the user-space Audit daemon. Additional user-space Audit utilities communicate with the kernel Audit element, Audit log files, and the Audit daemon.

- The auditctl (Audit control) utility communicates with the kernel Audit element for managing the rules along with controlling the parameters and settings of the event generation procedure.

189

- The other Audit utilities manage the contents of the Audit log files by using them as an input to produce output as per the user requirements. Like the `aureport` (Audit report), the utility can produce a report covering all the recorded events.

Audit Configuration

The predefined `auditd` configuration can be used for securing a wide majority of environments. Even so, many organizations require stringent security policies that can be achieved by modifying the `/etc/audit/auditd.conf` file with the following Audit daemon configurations.

- **`log_file`**

  It is recommended to always store the directory with the Audit log files (mostly `/var/log/audit/`) on a different mount point. This results in prohibiting other processes to consume additional space in that particular directory. It also precisely analyzes the free space for the Audit daemon.

- **`max_log_file`**

  This parameter mentions the largest size of a single Audit log file. It is important to set the parameter to ensure complete usage of the available space in the partition that stores the Audit log files.

- **`max_log_file_action`**

  The parameter determines the action to be executed as the limit in `max_log_file_action` is attained. To avoid overwriting the Audit log files, the parameter must be set to *keep_logs*.

- **space_left**

  This defines the remaining space on the disk and based on it, the space_left_action parameter gets triggered. It should be configured to a number that allows the admin to have a suitable time to take action by optimizing the disk space. The value of this parameter is reliant on the generation rate of the Audit log files.

- **space_left_action**

  The advisable configuration would be to configure this parameter to *exec* or *email* with a suitable notification system.

- **admin_space_left**

  This defines the very least amount of available space and based on it the admin_space_left_action parameter gets triggered. It should be configured to an appropriate value that allows the admin to execute log actions.

- **admin_space_left_action**

  In order to apply the single-user mode to the system, this parameter must be set to *single*, which will enable the admin to free the required amount of storage space.

- **disk_full_action**

  It defines a process that is triggered during unavailability of any free space on the partition storing the Audit log files. The parameter should be set to *single* or *halt*. This will make sure that the system either operates in single-user mode while there is no event logging by Audit, or the system shuts down entirely.

- **disk_error_action**

  The parameter defines the process that gets triggered when an error is identified on the system that stores the Audit log files. It should be set to *single*, *halt*, or *syslog*, based on the local security policies that manage the hardware malfunction situations.

- **flush**

  The flush parameter operates in synergy with the freq parameter, which controls the amount of records that can be directed to the disk, prior to a hard synchronization is forced with the hard drive. For optimized results, the flush parameter must be set to *incremental_async* while the freq parameter, to *100*. The parameters provide assurance that there is proper synchronization between event data and the log files stored on the disk, all while ensuring that better performance for activity bursts is maintained.

All the other options or parameters for configuration can be set as per the local security policies of the system.

Log entries are prestored in the file /var/log/audit/audit.log by the Audit system. When log rotation is set, rotated audit.log files are saved in the same directory.

By configuring the following additional Audit rule, all access and modification attempts of the /etc/ssh/sshd_config file will be logged.

```
# auditctl -w /etc/ssh/sshd_config -p warx -k sshd_config
```

To create a new event in the Audit log file when the auditd daemon is executed, use the following command:

```
$ cat /etc/ssh/sshd_config
```

Evaluate Vulnerabilities and Verify Compliance

Most of the cyber-attacks occurring worldwide are a result of overlooked and unpatched security vulnerabilities that include weak passwords and system configurations, web application exploits, and inept end-users' awareness. All such reasons make it very crucial to incorporate vulnerability evaluation or vulnerability assessment as an absolute requirement in every organization.

However, there are still many who carry out this security task for the mere purpose of complying with the standards and policies, failing to realize the threats posed to their mission-critical services and their own business.

Secure environments can also have some vulnerabilities, like in their network or system infrastructure. To overcome these security challenges, numerous organizations utilize vulnerability assessment tools that do the job for them. These tools usually detect plenty of minuscule vulnerabilities, rating them as per their severity, but more often than not the tools do not take into consideration the business impact and productivity downtimes.

To achieve a truly effective vulnerability assessment strategy and verify compliance, you would need to gain a comprehensive understanding of the critical processes and base infrastructure of your organization. The actions mentioned below will assist you with that.

Unprompted Active Role Partaking

When a vulnerability assessment is conducted, you can voluntarily consider taking a positive approach toward identifying the current state of the security system. If you are responsible for carrying out or supervising the task, you must do your proper research during screening the potential vendors or consultants, scoping procedure, and later help them with all the required data and accesses that will help achieve better results. Management should also participate in such activities as much as they can since it is also important for them to be aware of and acknowledge the security issues and challenges faced, as well as strategies implemented to resolve them.

193

Identifying the Key Business Processes

It is important to learn and understand all the processes involved with compliance, security, privacy, SDLC, and infrastructure. You can always go through the SOPs related to the aspects you want to learn more about. No one employee or team can handle all these aspects by themselves; they need multiple teams or individuals actively working together in synergy to achieve the desired results. The most important part of this process is to collaborate with the experts associated with each domain and factor in their recommendations. Their expertise holds significance as it might help other teams save time, efforts, and costs with the strategy to be implemented.

Zero In on Critical Applications Underneath the Processes

After the key business processes are identified and ordered as per their criticality, a later part will be to identify the data and applications those processes are reliant on. This process will help analyze which applications are actually critical as per separate domain requirements. For example, a CI application might be very critical for the DevOps team while being entirely futile for the network team.

Identify the Hardware Powering the Applications and Processes

After the previous two actions, the next step would be to work down the infrastructure layer by identifying the hardware that these applications are hosted or run on. Most common ones include physical and virtual servers, network devices, storage drives, firewalls, IDS/IPS, and so on. Access controls to these hardware (and applications) must be restricted to authorized personnel only.

Mapping Network Architecture

Observe and learn about the network infrastructure components like routers, switches, and firewalls, as the system connections are usually routed through these devices. It will also help you determine if any particular subnets are being utilized so as to maintain privacy over sensitive assets and data, like Domain Controllers, Active Directories, any application server, or if any VLANs are created to bifurcate the critical departments and their data.

Analyze the Security and Control Measures

All the security measures that are implemented in the organization must have documentation like an SOP or a brief overview. They can comprise standards, policies, accessibility, physical and virtual controls - more so with respect to network devices such as firewalls, IDS/IPS, VPNs, storage drives, DLP (Data Loss Prevention), servers, and so on. All such controls should be evaluated, and the vulnerabilities associated with each of them must be addressed. This process is one of the core elements of the *defense-in-depth* strategy that is implemented by many top-tier organizations.

Perform Vulnerability Scans

After having gone through the earlier mentioned actions, performing a vulnerability assessment scan of the systems will be most beneficial. With an extensive knowledge of all the systems, processes, applications, and the network architecture, you will be able to analyze and consider remediations more efficiently. It will also help you detect false positives more accurately, which are quite common while using security tools. After the remediation or patching, you will need to perform a vulnerability scan again so as to verify the successful patching of the system.

Consolidate the Scan Results with Technological and Business Context

Security tools conduct the scans and deliver results based on the technical vulnerabilities and their severities. It fails to consider other crucial factors, which is where your input will come to be valuable. Determining the business risk by analyzing the vulnerability scan results is essential in remediating the findings. Although the severity factors make it clear which vulnerabilities hold the highest priority, you have to consolidate those results with the potential business impact any of those resolutions might have and if/how much productivity could be hampered due to it.

The latest security tools also recommend the actions that can be executed to resolve those vulnerabilities. However, often you have to diligently evaluate those recommendations to decide if you have a better alternative as a solution. For example, in case of XSS vulnerabilities, tools might most likely suggest an update or patch to the current modules, which would act more like a temporary solution. You could instead deploy a WAF (Web Application Filter) to resolve all web-based vulnerabilities more effectively. Similarly, network vulnerabilities can be resolved by creating a DMZ (Demilitarized Zone), which guards the private and critical business network against various threats and exploits of the external network like the internet.

Perform Penetration Testing

After the vulnerability assessment is done, and all the necessary remediations have been taken to resolve those issues, the eventual step would be to conduct penetration testing. Performing a PT would give an organization detailed insight into whether a malicious user could gain unauthorized access to your system and steal/modify any data from it. Such potentially severe attacks can be replicated during a penetration testing that will allow you to verify the existence of any vulnerability and how it can be leveraged or exploited.

These are generally conducted by third-party vendors or consultants since their expertise and impartiality could be favorable during an audit. The vulnerability assessment and penetration testing reports are required to be presented during an audit (if there is such a requirement as per standard compliance regulations).

Evaluating vulnerabilities and verifying compliance can be considered two sides of the same coin. The amount and severity of the findings are also directly proportional to the compliance with standards, policies, and procedures. If the reports reflect minimum findings that too with minor severities, that will imply that the organization is doing its best to comply with all the security standards and predefined policies.

Conclusion

Not all tasks can be automated and especially in the security domain, roles like the system and network administrators, cyber analysts, DevOps engineers and similar play a very important role in securing the environments. That said, management and administration also play a key role in devising and implementing efficient security policies and strategies encompassing all relevant aspects. CISOs, IT teams, and infosec teams have the authoritative capabilities to ensure the compliance of security standards and implement optimum strategies to prevent and mitigate risks.

CHAPTER 7

Case Studies

Instead of sharing plenty of light case studies with similar scenarios and remediations, three primary case studies have been handpicked, showcasing different attack vectors and appropriate resolutions. Due to confidentiality and sensitivity issues, one of the case studies is kept anonymous, but the attacks are depicted as accurately as possible.

Case Study 1: Anonymous
Context

An employee of AZ1 Inc. had carried a personal laptop into the company premises. As it turned out, the laptop was infected with *Poison Ivy* trojan, which the employee was unaware of. After it was connected with the company network through a wireless access point, the laptop system was assigned an IP address from DHCP. The infected system established a connection to the command and control center (anony.mous.xyz.com) through the internet. The threat actor executed the command to make the system perform scanning of the local network to discover all the available services. Despite observing a performance dip on the system, the user casually ignored it, probably having been in a Friday weekend vibe. The system was left still connected while the user decided to scrutinize it on Monday. The conducted scan discovered an FTP service running on the private network that permitted anonymous access. The threat actor that

© Rithik Chatterjee 2021
R. Chatterjee, *Red Hat and IT Security*,
https://doi.org/10.1007/978-1-4842-6434-8_7

was still in control of the compromised system was able to log in to the FTP server, thereby compressing all the existing data and transferring it over to the control server via a VPN tunnel.

Across the weekend, the NOC (Network Operations Center) eventually tracked huge data content across an encrypted channel. Both the source and destination addresses were identified but since they did not have the decryption keys, they failed to decrypt the data and analyze any content. The source was obviously an IP from their private corporate network, the destination, however, was unidentified as it did not match from the list of malicious sites, which seemed valid as the list was outdated by over four months. A work ticket was then opened by the help desk to facilitate an investigation by the local desktop services.

The aforementioned user detected that in spite of a reboot, the compromised system was still unstable. A ticket for the same was opened after the user notified the help desk about the issue. With further analysis, the technician was able to match the IP address of the system to the unknown traffic investigated earlier. While physically rechecking, the technician deduced that the particular system was not an official corporate system and thus did not have the required security programs. Performing a quick scan through a boot time tool revealed *Poison Ivy* signature as the culprit. The system was immediately seized for an in-depth forensic investigation and the pending tickets were closed.

Through an exhaustive analysis of the system by the forensics team, the threat was confirmed to be *Poison Ivy*, a known malware tool. A temporary file was also detected that was actually a remnant of the initial scan containing the FTP site in its findings. A lot of folders in that FTP site directory were named after former critically valuable programs. The files consisted of a list of parts, quotations, and proprietary drawings as well. It also included patents belonging to the former CEO of the corporation, along with some legal documents with details of purchases and program legalities.

Policies and Controls That Could Have Helped

BYOD (Bring Your Own Device) Policy

It is important for an organization to be in control of the devices that are connected to its network. If not, external devices might pose severe threats to the organization. Devices that are not authorized might not have the high-grade security implementations as per the corporate standards to ensure data security. Such systems could bypass the existing defense system of the organization. The following sub-controls could have prevented such an incident.

By using an automated discovery tool, AZ1 Inc. could have blocked access from the device, as soon as it connected to the corporate network. The system could either be completely blocked out or be moved over to a logically isolated VLAN that would prevent it from accessing any corporate resources while also notifying the network team about its unapproved connection.

DHCP is used to ease systems into gaining IP addresses faster and more efficiently. However, this could also sometimes prove risky when compared to the safer option of static addressing. The network could be configured to disallow systems from joining the network without correct addressing and subnet information. When using DHCP, its compensating controls must also be enabled that do not let external devices take advantage of it by accessing official resources.

Network-level authentication could also have played an obstructive barrier, preventing the compromised system from joining the network in the first place. The authentication methods can be either using credentials or through utilizing authentication certificates for the system.

Limit Network Port Access

This control is one of the crucial security measures that should be implemented to make sure that every port, service, or protocol has a valid purpose serving the business of an organization. The running services should always be updated to the latest version to patch any potential vulnerabilities. Idle ports can act as a gateway for malicious applications to make their way into the network, which is why unused ports must always remain closed.

Even while using RHEL, post the configuration of network services, it should be monitored to identify the ports that are listening to the network interfaces of the system. Either a command like #ss -i, #lsof -i or #netstat -an can be executed to request the system to provide a list of all the listening ports on the system, or the most effective technique to identify the listening ports on a network is by using a port scanner like nmap, which is also used by many cybersecurity analysts.

Safeguarding FTP Server

The data theft occurred by accessing the FTP server through an anonymous login. This might have been the most severe security misconfiguration leading the attack to be successful. Access to sensitive data should always be restricted to absolute essential and authorized users, so allowing access to the FTP server by logging in anonymously was like an invitation for attacks. Except for misconfiguration, another possible reason for this could be that no assessment was carried out that would have determined the existence of sensitive data on the server. With a proper assessment, either the data could have been migrated to secure storage or appropriate security controls be implemented on the server.

In this scenario, the FTP server itself was the primary vulnerability that was exploited. FTP servers usually use clear text for usernames and passwords, with no encryption whatsoever. If organizations perform periodic scanning and gather known port baselines, a better insight into what services are being used can be gained. Although FTP is not a default package on modern Windows Internet Information Services (IIS) installations anymore, it is often installed, exposing the system and network to be exploited through this weak protocol.

If FTP is highly necessary, it could either be run via an encrypted tunnel that would eliminate the vulnerability of cleartext credentials or, more secure formats of the protocol can be used, like SFTP or FTPS.

Defense Mechanisms

Boundary defense needs to be implemented that would analyze the traffic and its legitimacy, between internal and external networks.

In a scenario like the one mentioned, firewall rules should have been implemented that would have restricted the outbound connection that the compromised system made with its command and control center, while also alerting the network team. In the case of a Red Hat environment, SELinux and ACLs should always be configured properly, which will enforce the strict security rules that are defined. Passive malware might have been ineffective and controlled much earlier.

Another preventive measure is configuring the infrastructure to ensure the traffic passes through a proxy firewall. By this, traffic that could not be decrypted using the escrowed keys of the organization is deemed illegitimate. Through restricting encrypted traffic that is not authorized, data extrusion can be avoided.

Apart from firewalls, IPS and IDS should also be deployed in the network security architecture that does a better job at blocking any malicious data in traffic. Based on the predefined rules on them, malware signatures or similar threats in the traffic are detected and immediately blocked while logging and alerting the administrators. In the above scenario, if either an IPS or IDS had been set up and configured properly, the incident could have been entirely prevented.

Data Security

One of the critical aspects of data security is locating sensitive data storage and restricting its access to only the required users. Along with this backup and recovery, it is also very essential for security purposes, too, as the backup systems provide security by copying or moving the sensitive data from a particular location to a more secure repository like the cloud or an offsite data center.

One of the best methods to protect sensitive data is by implementing DLP (Data Loss Prevention) solutions. Although conventional DLP solutions are host oriented, modern ones can monitor the network traffic, detecting anomaly variations. This will enable the DLP program to restrict any data export outside the corporate network as soon as any unidentified encrypted traffic is detected on an outbound connection, by the DLP sensor.

Whether or not a DLP solution is implemented, critical data must always be in an encrypted format. Data is generally classified into two types: at rest and in motion. Both types of data need this encryption before writing into a disk to ensure that only authorized users with the decryption key can access it.

Wireless Access Security

Cyber-attacks through wireless are one of the most common attack vectors in most organizations. Setting up wireless devices to provide convenience to employees, without comprehending the associated risks with it, places the entire organization and its users in grave risk. Just like in this case, users might casually connect their compromised devices to the network because they are already aware that connecting via wireless is no hassle. That is what exposes the network and its underlying vulnerabilities that are eventually exploited.

One of the methods to restrict network access is by implementing MAC-binding. This will allow only the systems with specific MAC addresses (that are defined in the network configuration) to connect to the network. A MAC address is assigned to an IP address and all the requests from that IP address are handled by the system with the assigned MAC address.

If ease of access is required for guest or client users, then creating and isolating the guest network from the main network maintains the optimum security. This way even if a malicious system is connected to the network, no harm can be done to the primary network and its users.

In the above scenario, after the incident came into light and the forensic investigation was over, CISO and the senior management of AZ1 Inc. were briefed with the reports. The CISO was instructed by the CEO to implement new and secure controls and update the existing ones. If only such steps were taken before, perhaps the incident could have been averted.

Case Study 2: Sony Pictures Entertainment (2014)

Context

One of the worst cyber-attacks to have occurred with a multinational corporation was initiated when a casual joke about making a comedy regarding the assassination of North Korean leader *Kim Jong-un* was made by actor *Seth Rogen* and screenwriter *Evan Goldberg*. This joke evolved into reality as in 2013 Sony Pictures Entertainment made the announcement about a comedy movie called *The Interview* with the said plot, directed by *Rogen* and *Goldberg*. The movie was scheduled to be released in 2014, but an unfortunate incident halted their plan. The entire network of Sony Picture Entertainment was compromised and attackers had gained control over it. Over 100 terabytes of data were stolen and made public on the internet that consisted of social security numbers, salaries, movies, along with personal information. This eventually forced Sony to take down its network and go offline.

Days later, an email meant for Sony Pictures CEO *Michael Lynton*, Chairman *Amy Pascal*, and other executives, was received. It referred to the "great damage" done to Sony and also demanded "monetary compensation" to prevent further defacement. Within three days, a Reddit post mentioned the occurrence of a breach at Sony Pictures Entertainment that was also responsible for bringing their entire internal and national network down. The post also mentioned that the attack was executed by a group called the GOP (Guardians of Peace). The group of hackers was claiming to be in possession of an enormous load of sensitive and critical data derived from the attack on Sony, supposedly on a scale of around 100 terabytes of data, which was gradually being publicized in bundles.

The stolen data also included usernames, passwords, confidential information regarding the network architecture of Sony, and several documents that exposed personal data of the employees. Following this, during December 2014, a classified *flash* alert was conveyed to many American organizations by the FBI, warning them about a harmful malware attack '*Wiper*' that had lately been executed. The said alert had left out the name of any victim, but many infosec experts concluded that the malware attack in question was congruous with the malicious code utilized in the latest attack on Sony.

The public and government of the USA claimed and alleged North Korea of its involvement in the attack that crippled Sony. North Korea however, denied all allegations regarding the attack, yet seemed rejoiced with the recent turn of events. The complete details of the attack on Sony are incomplete as certain internal aspects still remain undisclosed.

Later the USA and FBI both declared that the attack was indeed carried out by North Korea following which the CEO of Sony Pictures Entertainment posted a memo to the entire staff, providing confirmation about their compromised information. In spite of all the issues, after a lot of reconsiderations, the movie was eventually released in theaters. Having said that, the technicians from Sony did have to go through a lot of tedious work during the rebuilding of the network and bring it back online, after having been offline for weeks.

Policies and Controls That Could Have Helped

Encryption

Sony was robbed of around 100TB of data from their servers that consisted of critical information like usernames, passwords, social security numbers, emails, network details, movies, and more. One of the most mandatory aspects of the critical controls is data security, whether, internal or exported, at rest or in motion. This is primarily achieved through encryption. In the case of Sony, data being publicized was surely an unfortunate event, but if proper enterprise-grade encryption had been implemented, it might have been a lot more difficult, if not unlikely, for the attackers to decode the encrypted data.

Network Security

Through installing an automated network discovery tool, it can be configured to monitor critical information, certain keywords, and chosen document attributes. This would alert the network team in case of any forced attempts intended for data extrusion so that such connections can immediately be terminated and blocked. If Red Hat systems are deployed in your infrastructure, then Red Hat Satellite can be used to identify network hosts that are not part of the Satellite inventory, thus receiving an intimation about the connected hosts.

The *Wiper* malware could also have been planted through an external device, which is something that could be detected via constant network monitoring through automated network tools.

In the above scenario with Sony, during the execution of 100TB data theft by the GOP, an enormous amount of network traffic must have been produced. If essential network controls would have been in place, even a fragment of that traffic would have alerted the administrators and the event could have been prevented. By persistent monitoring through an automated network tool, any critical data being suspiciously exported from the corporate network could have been highlighted, thereby helping Sony gain control of the situation while it was still possible.

Usually encrypted channels are used to carry out such cyber-attacks, as it helps the attackers elude the existing network security. These situations nullify the security implementations, which is why it is very crucial to be able to detect rogue or malicious communication channels or connections and terminate them while resolving any compromised systems. If Sony would have been able to detect the creation of a potential covert channel, it would have notified them about the attack.

Data Scanning

By frequently scanning the network and servers, sensitive and critical data that is stored in clear text can be identified. Scan tools, especially those that work on a pattern or anomaly-based algorithms, are quite effective with their scans that pick out the existence of unencrypted data. Such tools also help in finding processes and applications that can potentially be exploited, leading to a data breach.

Using similar tools, it was possible for Sony to scan their servers to identify critical data stored in clear text format. As mentioned earlier, encrypting important data might have prevented the damage entirely or at least up to an extent, but targeted encryption can only be done if you know which data needs to be highly secured.

Malware Defense Mechanisms

As per reports from multiple security experts, the *Wiper* malware was used in the data theft attack on Sony in 2014. The malware derives its name from its functionality of wiping off data from the drives of its victims. It is absurd to think that the security or network team of Sony remained completely unaware of the installation of this malware. If the dropper and its installation files could have been detected before or even during the attack, a catastrophic data loss might have been averted. This proves how important it is to implement appropriate malware detection and defense mechanisms.

Anti-malware tools that are network oriented detect executables throughout the network, and modern tools do not just rely on signature-based detection. Patterns and abnormalities are analyzed that filter the threat prior to its arrival at the endpoint. The same could have helped Sony, especially while detecting unusual operations in its network infrastructure, caused by a malicious executable.

In Red Hat, enterprise-grade security is provided in the OS and the packages. Upon the detection of any security concerns regarding any applications, updated packages are provided to reduce the potential risk. If anti-malware is still deemed necessary, then either of the following tools can be installed and utilized because of their effectiveness and efficiency.

- chkrootkit

- rkhunter

- ClamAV

Data Recovery

After the occurrence of any severe business-critical events, the SOP related to disaster recovery that the organization has charted has to be followed. The major aspect of it includes restoring the affected systems as soon as possible by resolving the network issues and recovering data from reliable backups.

To follow this procedure, administrators need to make sure that systems are periodically backed up in an automated manner: the recommended time frame is at least once a week. While systems that store important data should be modified on a regular basis, daily backups would be more suitable.

For a proper and systematic restoration, the backup must include data, OS, and application software in the general backup process. All the three elements may or may not be part of the same backup file, however. Backups should be stored in multiple progressive versions so that if one of the files is corrupted, other ones can be used, or in case of a malware/virus attack, the systems can be restored from a specific version that assumably precedes the original infection.

The location where the backup files are stored needs to be properly secured as well, virtually or physically. Encryption is always the best solution, but security measures apart from that should also be applied, whether it be cloud services or a remote/local data center.

Sony's network was seriously damaged, which forced them to stay offline for weeks. The organization had to incur financial losses during that time. With organized backups, they could have been able to restore their network and systems much earlier, thus potentially saving some of those losses.

While using Red Hat systems, the Relax-and-Recover (ReaR) solution can be used for backup and recovery purposes, which is provided by default. ReaR is basically a system migration and recovery tool that generates a bootable image as a backup and this image is later used for system recovery. As this tool also allows the backup to be restored to different hardware, it can be utilized as a migration utility as well.

Administrative Privileges

One of the common methods of bypassing the security is through unauthorized or misuse of administrative access. Taking control over just one account can allow the attackers to escalate the required privileges and exploit the system.

Normal authentication is no longer considered safe, more so for organizations and their administrative and management access inclusive of domain accessibility. It is important to implement multifactor authentication with different methods like biometrics, smart cards, OTP, authenticator applications, and more.

When the GOP executed the attack on Sony, the subpar security of Sony had allowed the attackers to set valid credentials within the malware. This provided them with an increased probability of advancing across the infrastructure. Had supplementary authentication like multifactor or at least 2FA been implemented for the administrative accounts, access to sensitive information could have been secured.

Security Logging

Due to a lack of proper control measures regarding security analysis and event logging, perpetrators were able to mask their location along with their activities on the systems and the malicious application.

This could have been secured by setting up and configuring log analytics tools that helped with the accumulation of the logs and consolidating them. Logs from different systems are collected, correlated, and analyzed. Deploying such logging or SIEM (Security Incident and Event Management) tools enable system administration and the security teams to formulate event profiles that would help with the fine-tuning of event detection based on unusual patterns and anomalies. This prevents the occurrence of false positives and provides quick event detection, leaving analysts to assess better.

This technique could have been utilized by Sony to detect its infrastructure breach by analyzing the activities and comparing the variation from their predefined baseline. It is crucial to determine the normalcy of an infrastructure environment so as to be alerted and identify any threats or abnormal activities.

Accessible and efficient logging is one of the essential attributes of every Red Hat system, which is why most organizations prefer RHEL for their main servers. However, as there are multiple components as part of the infrastructure, it is important to simplify the debugging procedure by centralizing the logging in a hybrid or cloud environment. The `rsyslog` is recommended to be used which can serve as either a centralized server for logging or configure specific systems to transmit their logs to this server, often referred to as remote logging. This acts as a very good solution for security logging that can be used in various environments.

Network Segmentation

This aspect was mentioned in the previous case study too. Segmenting the network of an organization into different zones delivers higher control over the systems and its accessibility. This division also acts as a defense barrier, protecting the remaining network, systems, and sensitive data.

It is unclear whether Sony had different network zones, but if this measure was appropriately implemented by segmenting the systems and securing them with required security controls, the damage might have been contained or the impact could have been reduced.

Penetration Testing and Red Team Assessments

In order to be accustomed to threats and vulnerabilities and be equipped to handle various attack vectors or exploits, organizations need to conduct Red Team assessments and penetration tests. This will test the security limits of the infrastructure.

By conducting periodic third-party and internal penetration tests, organizations can detect their existing vulnerabilities and be exposed to the attack techniques that are usually used in cyber-attacks. It is always recommended to perform both: a black box penetration testing that is carried out from outside the network (just like an external malicious attacker would), and a white box or gray box testing in which the network and systems are tested with complete or partial knowledge of the corporate network (to emulate internal attack vectors).

Red Team assessments are identical to penetration testing in more ways than one, except the major difference is that these are more target oriented. Unlike penetration tests, the primary objective of Red Team assessments is not to identify the maximum number of vulnerabilities but instead to examine the threat identification and response proficiency of the organization. By conducting Red Team assessments, organizations can test the utmost limits of their infrastructure security, drastically reducing the chances of any potential attacks for that period.

As not many internal details regarding the attack on Sony are disclosed, it can only be assumed that either such security testing activities were not conducted periodically or if conducted, they were not up to the mark. Regardless, Sony should have instituted action items helping them mitigate severe risks. This would have suppressed or restrained the attack vector used by the attackers.

Incident Response

In the data breach attack on Sony, the attackers wiped off data from their systems as well as stole and publicized the data that included unreleased movie clips, private information of people, and some critical documents too. Sony failed to deploy an efficient and reliable incident response team during the course of the attack.

Organizations often fail to take into consideration the importance of security activities like incident scenario sessions. By performing such recurring sessions with the incident response team, existing threats, ways to handle them, and associated responsibilities can be managed in a better way.

The damages Sony incurred were not just limited to the data breach attack; the way they failed to recover from that attack quickly and effectively also contributed to their loss. If they would have conducted such incident response sessions, their aftermath damages could have been significantly reduced. Later after that attack, Sony Pictures Entertainment started deploying the latest systems and automated tools and then set up and configured enterprise-grade security controls. All these actions were implemented around forty days after the attack originally occurred. This delayed timeline proved how ineffective and disorganized their incident response activities were.

This attack on Sony is still considered to be one of the major cybersecurity incidents to have occurred in recent times. It managed to expose the security flaws and shortcomings of a world-renown and top-tier organization like Sony. The company was left in shambles while being inept in bringing their network back online and managing the enormous sensitive data leak, simultaneously. This case is evidence of the fact of how thorough an IT security architecture needs to be, right from the precautionary measures, up to incident management and data recovery.

Case Study 3: Capital One (2019)
Context

Capital One is a bank holding corporation originating from the United States that specializes in banking, loans, and credit cards. It is the fifth-biggest consumer bank in America and the eighth biggest bank in general, having around fifty thousand employees and a revenue of 28 billion US dollars in 2018.

Most banks around the world have their private data centers that host their entire infrastructure, including all the data. Capital One was among the initial banks in the world to migrate their on-prem infrastructure to a cloud computing service, which is where the attack was targeted. The cloud service was Amazon Web Service and the 'Capital One Migration' attack is listed by Amazon as a prominent case study. Capital One had already been utilizing the cloud computing environments for their core financial services and were jointly working with AWS to create a security model to facilitate improved security operations and complete the migration process by 2020. Even risk frameworks were built for the cloud environments prior to every workload migration, to ensure optimum compliance and security, similar to that of their on-prem infrastructure.

In July 2019, Capital One revealed that they suffered a data breach in which a third-party individual had managed to gain access to their server. As per their public report, this outside individual had acquired unauthorized access and stole sensitive data like some personal information of Capital One credit card customers. The personal information included names, phone numbers, addresses, zip codes, email addresses, birthdates, and self-reported incomes. The breach had compromised around 100 million people in the United States and around 6 million in Canada as well, comprising consumer data from individuals and small enterprises.

The incident was detected on July 17, 2019, by the Responsible Disclosure Program of Capital One itself, rather than being exposed by usual cybersecurity operations. As per the FBI complaint lodged with a US District Court at Seattle, an email from an unknown individual was received by Capital One that informed them regarding their data being publicly available on a GitHub page. Capital One later clarified that a part of the data that was stolen had been in an encrypted format. However, they also mentioned that because of an exception in this incident, the unauthorized access managed to aid the decryption of data.

After the arrest of a woman from Seattle, named *Paige A. Thompson,* related to this hacking incident, it was discovered that she used to work for Amazon, which made it evident that the servers she had accessed were hosted on AWS (Amazon Web Services). She had also stolen data from 30 or more organizations through a software scanning tool that she had created. Using the tool she could discover servers hosted in the cloud computing service that was secured with misconfigured firewalls. This enabled her to execute commands for penetrating and accessing the servers, without connecting to any of their networks.

In the FBI investigations, a GitHub hosted script was discovered that was used to access the data within Capital One cloud servers. The script file had three commands through which it facilitated the unauthorized access to their server hosted on AWS. The execution of the initial command acquired the security credentials, which was used to access the folders of Capital One. The second command listed the folder and data bucket names saved in the storage space of Capital One. The third command was used to copy these data stored in the data buckets and folders. The biggest security flaw was the firewall misconfiguration that allowed these commands to be executed in the server of Capital One, thereby providing access to the data stored within it. Apart from this, the FBI also claimed that Capital One even verified through their system logs and the commands were indeed executed.

The reports were analyzed and it was concluded that the vulnerable server was accessible due to an SSRF (Server-Side Request Forgery) attack that could be performed because of a misconfiguration in the WAF (Web Application Firewall) deployed in the infrastructure of Capital One. (In SSRF attacks servers are deceived to make them connect to a different server than the one originally intended, forcing them to generate a request that is controlled by the attacker. The attack takes place especially when web applications need external resources, which allows the attackers to transmit customized requests from a vulnerable web app's back-end server.)

Policies and Controls That Could Have Helped

Firewall Configurations

In the attack on Capital One, the TOR network was used to mask the location of the attack origin. Firewall rules should always be configured properly that block host access and IP addresses originating from the TOR network, malicious proxy servers, and exit nodes too. Granted that not all suspicious IP addresses can be blocked, but setting up rules that alert the administrators during unusual activities from such IPs can be configured. Along with firewalls, IPS or IDS rules and alerts also need to be configured as they have a higher chance of detecting and terminating connections from malicious IPs.

Capital One could have set up network monitoring through which they could have detected the attack during its occurrence itself. While migrating their on-prem infrastructure to the cloud, monitoring third-party cloud service providers and all activities related to it, should have been given more priority. An absence of this created a security loophole with regard to monitoring that otherwise could have been prevented.

The primary contributor to this attack was the WAF misconfiguration that allowed the successful execution of those commands. In the case of cloud infrastructure and hosted web applications, WAF plays an important role. Often these configurations are just left at their default settings and rules, which have their obvious flaws.

Errors in configurations of WAF can be detected through preventive vulnerability scans. Conducting frequent vulnerability scans can help identify such errors and other issues and vulnerabilities as well. Based on this, Capital One should have also created vulnerability management plans that would have helped them handle these issues.

For instance, RHEL comes with a preinstalled vulnerability scanner called OpenSCAP. SCAP stands for Security Content Automation Protocol and is a specification framework supporting automated configuration, verification of vulnerabilities and patches, compliance activities, along with security measures. OVAL (Open Vulnerability Assessment Language) is the core and oldest element of SCAP and its declarative attribute restricts unprecedented modifications to the assessed system state. Tools like OpenSCAP combined with RHSA OVAL definitions ensure maintaining higher security and providing vulnerability scan reports.

Access Controls

It is crucial for organizations to monitor and audit the usage of admin accounts. The data within the Capital One server was stolen after accessing it through the credentials required for it. This case proves again how essential multifactor authentication is, especially to secure the administrative accounts.

The principle of least privilege and segregated duties should be practiced. This way escalated privileges can be provided only if absolutely required and only for a specific time period. All credentials that are issued for different accounts need to be verified and revoked if necessary, and all of these should be audited to identify any security shortcomings related to accessibility.

Encryption

Throughout most of the case studies available online, encryption will remain one of the most common security controls that is recommended to be implemented. If all the sensitive data is encrypted, it acts as the last line of defense against attacks. Even if the data gets stolen, without decrypting it, its content cannot be accessed.

In the case of Capital One, they claim to have encrypted the data but this exceptional scenario enabled the attacker to also be able to decrypt the data after gaining access to the server. The exact details pertaining to this attribute are unclear, so it can only be assumed that the decryption keys or the privileges required to decrypt the data were granted to the account, the credentials of which were used to access the server. Although this remains just speculation, this factor still needs due consideration as you are now well aware of its potential misuse. To prevent privilege escalation, duties should be separated and all access activities have to be monitored, either through an automated tool or manually.

To overcome the shortcoming of default encryption, Red Hat has infused OpenShift to be used in FIPS (Federal Information Processing Standards) mode that provides a consistently secure environment. As mentioned in the OpenShift architecture section of Chapter 2, OpenShift also allows users to encrypt their sensitive data, preventing unauthorized accesses.

Monitoring

One of the key reasons that this attack was successfully executed and discovered only until later was because there was a lack of proper logging and monitoring. This aspect has been emphasized multiple times before, but organizations usually tend to ignore the significance of monitoring. Even administrators sometimes sidetrack routine monitoring activities. With modern tools and solutions, monitoring and logging can be entirely automated.

In the case of Capital One, their data was stored in folders and buckets on AWS S3 (Simple Storage Service). They should have utilized AWS CloudWatch that provides monitoring metrics and allows them to aggregate, access, and compare the data across all the AWS resources.

Red Hat Cloud Forms also works as a good alternative for automated tracking and monitoring of activities on your cloud infrastructure. It supports the creation of widgets, charts, and reports; and which by using, all the activities across your cloud environment can be tracked and monitored. Alerts can be created that will notify you via emails or SNMP traps whenever a custom-defined parameter or condition gets triggered. Policies, policy profiles, and alerts can also be imported so as to integrate them and use along with CloudForms Management Engine infrastructures.

The Capital One incident shows the significance of essential security controls even while using cloud infrastructure. Even though they followed most of the standard protocols and policies, a simple mistake of improper configuration led the attackers to successfully execute the attack.

Additional Case Studies

There are many more cybersecurity cases that managed to rattle the IT industry, considering the magnitude of the impact those attacks had on the organizations, employees, and common people alike. These case studies were not chosen to be mentioned in detail as they were mostly related to web application security, other attack vectors, or the evidence was not disclosed properly to figure out the actual cause of the attack.

Bangladesh Bank Cyber Heist (2016)

Attackers were able to use SWIFT (Society for Worldwide Interbank Financial Telecommunication) credentials of employees of the Bangladesh Central Bank to transmit over three dozen deceitful requests for money transfers to the Federal Reserve Bank of New York and further make requests to transfer millions from the first bank to bank accounts situated in Sri Lanka, Philippines, and a few other Asian regions. Although the Bangladesh bank had managed to block $850 million of transaction requests, attackers were still able to rob them of $81 million. The attack was speculated to have been taken place either through an insider's help or due to lackluster security implementations at the Bangladesh bank that supposedly did not even have a firewall installed, allowing the attackers to bypass the authentication easily and retrieve the stored credentials. The attackers had also used a customized malware to try to cover their track, which was later detected.

Facebook–Cambridge Analytica Data Scandal (2018)

In this attack, personal data belonging to millions of Facebook users was procured without their permission, by a company called Cambridge Analytica. The app, which was initially made for psychological analysis of users, managed to harvest personal data of users and later on sell the data of the US citizens to political campaigns. It is said that the attackers used Facebook developer APIs to gain data that included name, gender, age, hometown and such, linking to the profile page of a user. The three bugs that lead to the attackers gaining access were the following: the 'View As' feature that allowed your profile to be displayed as it would to someone else, a video uploader bug, and an access token bug.

Twitter Hack (2020)

In July 2020, attackers were able to obtain access to the Twitter accounts of some of the most influential personalities including Bill Gates, Elon Musk, Apple, Warren Buffet, Jeff Bezos, Barack Obama, Mike Bloomberg, and a few more. A fake message asking people to donate bitcoins through a provided link was tweeted from all these accounts simultaneously, in a well-coordinated attack, eventually scamming people of around $121,000. Twitter described the main cause of the attack as Social Engineering, in which attackers fool or trick an internal employee into providing them with the accessibility credentials or some sensitive information. Although Twitter did not reveal many details, a report from *Vice* mentioned that after talking (anonymously) with some of the hackers involved in the attack, they claimed to have bribed a Twitter employee in order to obtain access to a particular tool that delivers deep control over high-profile Twitter accounts.

References

Red Hat:

https://access.redhat.com/documentation

https://access.redhat.com/knowledgebase

https://www.redhat.com/en/technologies

https://www.redhat.com/en/blog

https://docs.ansible.com/ansible

https://docs.openshift.com

https://kubernetes.io/docs

DevOps:

https://www.redhat.com/en/topics/devops

https://www.devsecops.org

IT and Cloud Security:

https://www.redhat.com/en/topics/cloud-computing

https://www.redhat.com/en/topics/security

https://resources.infosecinstitute.com/

https://aws.amazon.com/blogs/security/tag/cloud-security/

https://en.wikipedia.org/wiki/Cloud_computing_security

Case Studies:

https://www.sans.org/reading-room/whitepapers/casestudies/case-study-cis-controls-limit-cascading-failures-attack-36957

https://www.sans.org/reading-room/whitepapers/casestudies/case-study-critical-controls-sony-implemented-36022

http://web.mit.edu/smadnick/www/wp/2020-07.pdf

© Rithik Chatterjee 2021
R. Chatterjee, *Red Hat and IT Security*,
https://doi.org/10.1007/978-1-4842-6434-8

REFERENCES

https://en.wikipedia.org/wiki/Bangladesh_Bank_robbery

https://en.wikipedia.org/wiki/Facebook-Cambridge_Analytica_data_scandal

https://en.wikipedia.org/wiki/2020_Twitter_bitcoin_scam

Index

A

Access Vector Cache (AVC), 16
Adequacy audit, 180, 181
Agile development, 66, 67
Amazon Web Service (AWS),
     215, 216
Anonymous access
    aforementioned user, 200
    boot time tool, 200
    BYOD, 201
    conducted scan, 199
    data security, 204
    defense mechanisms, 203
    exhaustive analysis, 200
    infected system, 199
    laptop system, 199
    limit network port access, 202
    NOC, 200
    poison Ivy trojan, 199
    safeguarding FTP Server, 202
    source/destination
        addresses, 200
    threat actor, 199
    wireless access security, 204, 205
Application Performance
        Management (APM), 69
Application server, 10, 195
Availability principle, 21

B

Bangladesh Bank Cyber Heist, 220
Block-level storage, 15, 139
Bring Your Own Device (BYOD), 201
B-Tree File System, 14
Buffer overflow
    heap, 86
    stack, 86

C

Cambridge Analytica, 221
Capital One, 214
    access controls, 218
    AWS, 215, 216
    cloud computing
        environments, 215
    cloud computing service, 216
    data breach, 215
    encryption, 218, 219
    FBI investigations, 216
    firewall configurations, 217, 218
    GitHub page, 215
    monitoring, 219, 220
    reports, 216
    responsible disclosure
        program, 215
    script file commands, 216

Printed in the United States
By Bookmasters